# leading
from below the surface

# leading
## from below the surface

A Non-Traditional Approach to School Leadership

theodore creighton

**CORWIN PRESS**
A Sage Publications Company
Thousand Oaks, California

*For information:*

Corwin Press
A Sage Publications Company
2455 Teller Road
Thousand Oaks, California 91320
E-mail: order@corwinpress.com

Sage Publications Ltd.
1 Oliver's Yard
55 City Road
London, EC1Y 1SP
United Kingdom

Sage Publications India Pvt. Ltd.
B-42, Panchsheel Enclave
Post Box 4109
New Delhi 110 017 India

Printed in the United States of America

**Library of Congress Cataloging-in-Publication Data**

Creighton, Theodore B.
Leading from below the surface: a non-traditional
approach to school leadership/Theodore Creighton.
      p. cm.
Includes bibliographical references and index.
ISBN 0-7619-3952-0 (cloth) — ISBN 0-7619-3953-9 (pbk.)
   1. School principals. 2. School management and organization.
3. Educational leadership. 4. Decision making. I. Title.
LB2831.9.C74 2005
371.2'012-dc22

                                                    2004005726

This book is printed on acid-free paper.

04   05   06   07   08   09   10   9   8   7   6   5   4   3   2   1

| | |
|---|---|
| *Acquisitions Editor:* | Robert D. Clouse |
| *Editorial Assistant:* | Candice Ling |
| *Production Editor:* | Tracy Alpern |
| *Copy Editor:* | Teresa Herlinger |
| *Proofreader:* | Sue Irwin |
| *Typesetter:* | C&M Digitals (P) Ltd. |
| *Indexer:* | Sylvia Coates |
| *Cover Designer:* | Michael Dubowe |
| *Graphic Designer:* | Lisa Miller |

# Contents

# *Preface*

## WHAT THIS BOOK IS NOT ABOUT

This is not a traditional or theoretical book about leadership. As you know, the bookshelves are already full of every imaginable kind of book on leadership: transformational leadership, moral leadership, participatory leadership, and many others. Please understand, I am not critical of the existing literature on school leadership, and yes, we have much to learn from these models. But during my many years as a school principal and superintendent, and now a professor responsible for preparing effective school leaders, it is my observation and belief that effective school leadership does not often match what we espouse in preparation programs. I have also observed that preparing effective school leaders is not generally as complex or complicated as we posit.

I must admit that much of my position is based on the recent book of Joseph Badaracco (2002), *Leading Quietly*. As sometimes happens, we run across the writing of a great author, and we think, "That's exactly what I have been trying to say." This has been the case with my exposure to *Leading Quietly*. Though Badaracco talks about leadership in the corporate world, I argue that the same is true in situations requiring effective school leadership. Badaracco helped me understand that true leadership is not grand or heroic: It occurs in small steps by people guided by humility, practicality, and common sense. They have the ability to look well below what we see on the surface.

Though I present in Chapter 2 a review of leadership theory, this book is not grounded in organizational theory.

Rather, I present a conceptual framework *based* on organizational theory, emphasizing the importance of school leaders resisting the temptation to focus on just what we see on the surface and instead explore and investigate much further below the surface to get at the issues (and children) who are so often neglected or at best, only partially served.

## ACKNOWLEDGMENTS

Corwin Press gratefully acknowledges the contributions of the following individuals:

Patti L. Chance
Assistant Professor
University of Nevada
Las Vegas, NV

Pamela S. Flood
Assistant Professor
Florida State University
Tallahassee, FL

Douglas G. Hesbol
Superintendent
Thomasboro Grade School
    District 130
Thomasboro, IL

Kristina A. Hesbol
Assistant Professor
University of Illinois at
    Urbana-Champaign
Champaign, IL

Gina Segobiano
Superintendent/Principal
Signal Hill School
    District 181
Belleville, IL

Glenn Sewell
Superintendent/Principal
Wheatland High School
Wheatland, CA

Dana Trevethan
Principal
Turlock High School
Turlock, CA

Bill Zeller
Principal
Yuba City High School
Yuba City, CA

# About the Author

 **Theodore Creighton** is currently a Professor and Director of the Center for Research and Doctoral Studies in Educational Leadership at Sam Houston State University (SHSU), where he teaches courses in educational research, educational statistics, and program evaluation. His background includes teaching at various grade levels in Washington, DC; Cleveland, Ohio; and Los Angeles, California. His administrative experience includes serving as principal and superintendent in both Fresno and Kern Counties, California. He holds a master's degree in educational administration from Kent State University and a doctorate from the University of California, Davis.

Creighton is currently the Executive Director of the National Council of Professors of Educational Administration (NCPEA) and serves on the Commission for the Advancement of Educational Leadership Programs (NCAELP). He is also on the National Policy Board for Educational Administration. Creighton is widely published in educational leadership journals, and is the author of *Schools and Data: The Educator's Guide for Using Data to Improve Decision Making* and *The Principal as Technology Leader.*

## CHAPTER ONE

# *Introduction*

To thoroughly define "leading from below the surface," it is necessary to review the existing leadership theory in order to place this concept in perspective. This review is presented in Chapter 2. The theoretical/conceptual framework that is the primary focus of this book is shaped by the review and is provided at the end of that chapter. This leading-from-below-the-surface framework serves as a "connect" and ties the chapters together, keeping the attention on principal leadership skills in school practice. In Chapter 3, I then give my readers more detail and explanation of exactly what I mean by leading from below the surface.

Let me first provide a brief overview and specific definition of leading from below the surface.

## FIRST, WHAT IS THE SURFACE?

I suggest that for the most part, *surface* is synonymous with the obvious or clearly visible. As we attempt to positively impact teaching and learning, we see teachers delivering instruction in some pretty clear ways: direct instruction, collaborative learning groups, individual learning centers, use of technology to enhance learning, etc. And we spend most of our time observing this teaching in formal classroom situations. We are guided by clear goals and specific objectives, and we evaluate teachers systematically. Much learning takes place in these traditional classrooms. But to get below the surface, we must expand our thinking beyond the obvious and visible.

Looking at students and evidence of effective learning, we again focus on the more visible and obvious: test scores, attendance data, discipline referrals, and report card grades. Here lies an inherent danger of staying on or above the surface: We have a tendency to highlight the average and above-average students, missing some of the students who might be considered at risk of educational failure. The real attributes and successes of some students are not clearly revealed by test scores and report card grades. Again, we must look deeper to get at the complete meaning of effective learning.

To further identify the surface, let's visit our friends Bolman and Deal (1984). As you may know, they suggest four frames as approaches to better understand and manage organizations: (a) structural frame, (b) human resource frame, (c) political frame, and (d) symbolic frame. My below-the-surface model can be better understood if we think of the first two frames representing the surface, and the last two frames helping us to lead from below the surface.

Think for a moment about the first two frames: structural and human resource. If we look closely, we find that these two frames occur on the surface, or as Bolman and Deal (1984) explain, "the structural and human resource frames attend primarily to formal structure" (p. 235) and "represent the obvious sides of schools" (p. 234). The structural frame emphasizes the importance of structure: rules, policies, objectives, and management kinds of activities. The human resource frame involves the needs, feelings, and prejudices of teachers, students, and administrators in our schools. The often-repeated theme of *principal as instructional leader* is heavily emphasized by structural ideas, and centers on the structural and human resource frames. To better define my concept of leading from below the surface, let me highlight a portion of their discussion of these two frames:

> It is not that either of these perspectives is wrong; they are both quite useful in explaining how schools work or in developing policies and strategies for helping them to improve. The main problem is that each leaves something

out; that together they do not highlight significant features of schools as organizations. To capture the *hidden sides of schools,* we need to entertain other *less obvious* perspectives. (p. 235; emphasis mine)

It is these hidden sides of schools that I suggest we travel to in leading from below the surface.

## OK, Now What Does "Below the Surface" Mean?

Let's start with an example. In a recent program evaluation for the Klein Independent School District in Houston, Texas, I was asked to investigate the number of graduating seniors taking advanced math courses. When looking at the existing data, I noticed that 72% of the students graduating from the district's three high schools completed advanced math courses (Pre-Algebra, Algebra 1 and 2, Geometry, Trigonometry, Statistics, Pre-Calculus, and Calculus) during their high school career. The superintendent and board were very proud of this figure. But to the superintendent's credit, he requested that I look into the situation further. We both agreed that sometimes looking at a single statistic does not present the whole story or paint the complete picture.

Obviously, we wanted to look at issues of gender, ethnicity, race, and socioeconomic level. But more important, I wanted to investigate the completion rates as they corresponded to each of the individual math courses. Specifically, I wanted to report the highest math course that students completed. Something very interesting and significant *surfaced.* My findings are shown below.

We're sure glad we did not stop at the first data report, revealing a 72% completion rate. Sure enough, it is accurate, but as you see, it does not really complete the picture. This second bit of information suggested that the district needed to attend to some specific courses and specific groups of students.

In the process of our literature review, we uncovered the results of a similar study completed by the U.S. Department of

**Table 1.1**    Percent of Graduating Seniors by Highest
                Mathematics Course at Klein High School

| Highest Math Course Completed | % Seniors Completing |
| --- | --- |
| Pre-Algebra | 9% |
| Algebra 1 | 13% |
| Algebra 2 | 27% |
| Geometry | 18% |
| Trigonometry | 22% |
| Pre-Calculus | 11% |
| Calculus | 7% |
| Statistics | 9% |

Education, National Center for Educational Statistics, in 1995, representing graduating seniors across the nation. This information, shown in Table 1.2, was helpful in showing the Klein School District that there was nothing terribly wrong with their seemingly low figures. They were very close to the national figures. Though this was somewhat comforting to them, the superintendent still found his figures unacceptable and began to look at strategies for increasing the completion rates in Pre-Algebra, Algebra 1, and Algebra 2. His rationale was to improve the base courses in hopes that improvement would naturally occur in the more advanced courses.

We hear much these days about data-based decision making. I suggest we use different terminology to describe how principals lead from below the surface: *evidence-based decision making.* Many times (as in my example above) it is not enough to look just at the clear and obvious data. The data revealed a 72% completion rate, but looking at the *evidence* requires a broader and deeper (below the surface) investigation. The individual math course completion rate was much more meaningful and truly represented what was happening at Klein's three high schools.

As our visit with Bolman and Deal helped us with understanding the *surface,* they can also help us better understand *below the surface.* Let's go back to their four frames and focus on the last two: (a) political and (b) symbolic. In their discussion of

**Table 1.2**    Percent of Graduating Seniors by Highest
Mathematics Course Completed in High School

| Highest Math Course Completed | % of Seniors Completing |
| --- | --- |
| Less than Pre-Algebra | 8% |
| Pre-Algebra | 6% |
| Algebra 1 | 11% |
| Algebra 2 | 31% |
| Geometry | 14% |
| Other advanced math* | 21% |
| Calculus | 9% |

* Includes Algebra 3, Trigonometry, Pre-Calculus, and Probability and
Statistics

SOURCE: Department of Education, National Center for Education
Statistics (1995).

the *hidden sides of schools,* they state that political and symbolic
theories look at schools quite differently. Rather than advo-
cating rational control exercised through authority, a political
view concentrates on a negotiated order achieved through the
exercise of power among groups and coalitions (Peterson &
Wimpleberg, 1983). From a symbolic perspective (rituals, cere-
monies, stories, gossip), the elements of culture form the glue
that holds an organization together (Deal & Kennedy, 1982).

Some organizations have tangible products, allowing leaders to focus mostly on Bolman and Deal's structural and human
resource frames. But schools are much more complex, with
effective teaching and student learning representing more
intangible products. Because of this complexity, school leaders
must spend considerable time "hanging out" below the surface.

In a sense, leading from below the surface involves two significant dimensions: (1) expanding your decision making beyond
the formal and obvious places (i.e., classrooms) and (2) moving
from data-based decision making to a deeper perspective utilizing evidence-based decision making. Effective principals are
those who focus time and attention on each of these two areas.
They realize that very few significant decisions are made in the
principal's office or in meetings with the superintendent or board.

Effective principals make decisions in hallways with teachers, on school buses with children, in kitchens with cafeteria workers, on the ball field with coaches, and at the Tuesday evening Lion's Club meeting. Though these places are very visible and on the surface in their own right, the principal's presence there is *below the surface* in regard to where traditional leadership preparation suggests leadership takes place.

Let me finish this chapter with another example to help us understand leading from below the surface. Let's return to the Westside School District in California, but when I was serving as superintendent of the district. We received word from the State Department of Education that our application for building-restructuring monies had been approved. This meant that finally we would have the monies to refurbish our classrooms with state-of-the-art technology, new air conditioners (to replace our trusty old "swamp coolers"), fix the leaks with new roofs, put in new bathrooms, and meet all the rest of our construction needs. As you probably know, the superintendent of a small rural district is designated as the *owner* of a building construction or reconstruction project, monitoring architects, contractors, bids, change orders, and building inspectors. This role is all-consuming, requiring early morning meetings with architects and contractors, and after-hours meetings with board members.

In a very real sense, all of one's time in this situation takes place in Bolman and Deal's *structural* and *human resource* frames, and consists of the very obvious: working with established plans and procedures, interpreting contracts, inspecting completed work, staying on budget, and so on. I think you can begin to sense the difficulty that was lying ahead for me.

I found myself spending less and less time conferring with teachers and students. Busy with the reconstruction project, I began to neglect the more invisible and intangible aspects of leading the district. Often, I would have to designate classroom observations and the handling of staff meetings to the principal. Obviously, this was a great opportunity for the principal, as he became more and more responsible for instructional leadership. But for me, it meant not paying attention to the *political* and *symbolic* frames (below the surface).

The trouble ahead for me included (1) frustrated teachers who felt ignored and unsupported, (2) disappointed community members who missed the regular communication and contact with their superintendent, and (3) puzzled education officials who noticed my increased absence from county and state meetings and workshops. Needless to say, I discovered myself to be in a potentially dangerous situation. Superintendents can wake up any morning and (through no fault of their own) find that any of the three stakeholders mentioned above feel ignored, alienated, or left out of the decision-making process. Fortunately, for whatever reason, I was able to shift focus and get myself back to the *below-the-surface* issues. Part of the solution was to pull my principal into some of the decisions and meetings required with the reconstruction responsibilities. In addition, I solicited and invited more participation and involvement from individual board members with these duties, allowing me to return to some of the more invisible and intangible matters.

## LEADERSHIP IS BOTH OBJECTIVE AND SUBJECTIVE

A final suggestion to help us with the understanding of leading from below the surface is to look at the objective and subjective sides involved. We generally overemphasize the objective aspect of leadership: facts, data, and test scores. At the same time, leadership *is* subjective, in that it involves the feelings, beliefs, and values of others. The objective components of *on the surface* are, as stated earlier, visible and tangible. Charged with monitoring the building reconstruction, I rarely thought about anything but the visible and tangible: building plans, contracts, inspection codes, and all the other formal aspects of building construction. If we think for a moment of the dichotomy of leadership and management, I posit that I was doing a pretty good job of managing. But what about leading?

Leading from *below the surface* requires a principal or superintendent to address the subjective components of leadership: the more invisible and intangible things such as teachers' attitudes and beliefs, community members' feelings, and state and county educators' perceptions. Not until I returned to *below the surface* did I get back to the real essence of leading a school district.

In closing this chapter, allow me to suggest that leading from below the surface can be likened to an iceberg: Only 10% of the iceberg is seen above the surface of the water. It is the 90% of the iceberg that is hidden below the surface that most concerns the ship's captain who navigates the water. Like an iceberg, the most meaningful (and potentially dangerous, as I found out as superintendent during reconstruction) is the invisible or subjective part that is continually operating at the unconscious level, the part that shapes people's beliefs and perceptions (Cushner, McClelland, & Safford, 2003). It is this aspect of leadership that can be the most troublesome and potentially dangerous, and that requires the most attention and emphasis in effectively leading schools.

## CHAPTER TWO

# *What Does Traditional Leadership Look Like, and How Did We Get Here From There?*

The purpose of this chapter is to give a brief overview of the many different theories of or approaches to leadership. How would you complete this sentence? "Leadership is ... " I suggest there are as many ways to complete the sentence as there are individuals reading this chapter. In the past 50 years, there have been as many as 65 different classifications developed to define the dimensions of leadership (Fleishman et al., 1991, as cited in Northouse, 2004). Within these 65 classifications, there are several specific theoretical forms of leadership— situational leadership, transformational leadership, moral leadership, and so on. To further cloud the issue, we distinguish between leadership and management. Wow! Where do we go from here? Truly, leadership is a very complex phenomenon.

In taking you through a brief history of leadership theories and approaches, I want to follow a format presented by Peter Northouse in his recent (2004) edition of *Leadership:*

*Theory and Practice.* This format follows the classifications of leadership mentioned above, and within each classification there exist several different theories or models.

The point I want to make in this chapter is that, from my experience and perspective, I do not see leaders from below the surface following any of the specific theories. I am reminded of a quote from a world-renowned statistician related to theories and models:

"All models are wrong—but some are useful."

George E. P. Box
Professor Emeritus, University of Wisconsin

I agree that leaders have something to learn from the study of leadership theory. But I am suggesting that there are large numbers of effective school leaders who pay attention to and exhibit characteristics far removed from any of our established theories. Let me go on with my brief review of the literature.

In the early 1800s, leadership characteristics or "traits" were studied to determine what made certain people great leaders. For example, if we could identify the traits possessed by Abraham Lincoln, we could perhaps duplicate them in others. This "trait approach" was based on the belief that leaders were born with certain characteristics that made them great leaders and were different than others who were more passive followers. Examples of some of these traits included intelligence, self-confidence, self-determination, integrity, and sociability.

In the middle of the 20th century, many researchers (e.g., Stogdill, 1948) argued that no identifiable set of traits separated effective leaders from ineffective leaders. Leadership now began to emerge as a relationship between people and situations. This actually was the beginning of a theory that is now called situational leadership. Although it first surfaced in 1948, it is interesting to observe that we are currently revisiting the notion of situational leadership.

## BEHAVIORAL LEADERSHIP

Researchers, after realizing that trying to identify leadership traits or characteristics was not dependable, began to study leadership *behavior*. In other words, they wanted to observe individuals as they were actually leading an organization or group of people.

During the 1960s and early 1970s, two major research studies looked at the behavior of leaders: the Ohio State studies and the University of Michigan studies. The first study focused on asking employees to report the number of times their leaders displayed certain types of behavior. Two specific types of leadership behaviors surfaced: (a) behavior centered on structure and (b) behavior based on consideration. In other words, leaders provide *structure* for employees, and leaders *consider* or *care about* the people under them. The University of Michigan study revealed similar results, identifying two specific types of leadership behavior: (a) production oriented and (b) employee oriented. Production orientation involved completion of tasks and getting work done, paralleling the structure behavior found in the Ohio study. Employee orientation involved the display of strong human-relations skills and relationships with employees, aligning with the consideration behavior of the Ohio study.

In essence, these two studies indicated that effective leaders had to concern themselves with both task orientation and relationship orientation. The studies also found that some organizations might need leaders more focused on tasks while others might benefit from leadership with strong human-relations skills.

## SITUATIONAL LEADERSHIP

Hersey and Blanchard (1993) are credited with the development of the theory of situational leadership. In essence, *situational leadership theory* involves a different form of leadership for each different situation. The contention is that an effective

**Figure 2.1**    Directive and Supportive Behaviors

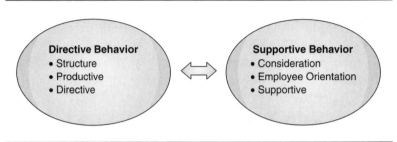

leader must adapt his or her style to the requirements of different situations. Interestingly, the two components of situational leadership (directive behavior and supportive behavior) again parallel the structure and consideration constructs identified in the Ohio State study and the production orientation and employee orientation of the Michigan study. Figure 2.1 shows such an alignment.

As you may notice, we are beginning to see the distinction between what we now consider as management behaviors (structure, production, directive) and leadership behaviors (consideration, employee orientation, supportive). Directive behaviors involve giving directions to organizational members, outlining goals and timelines, and methods of evaluation. On the other hand, leaders use supportive behaviors to help organizational members to feel good about themselves and to give them social and emotional support.

As popular as the Hersey/Blanchard theory is, little research has been completed giving evidence that applying the theory really does improve performance. Critics argue that the model does not adequately address "developmental levels" of subordinates. In addition, situational leadership theory does not fully address one-to-one versus group leadership in an organizational setting (Northouse, 2004, pp. 62–63).

## CONTINGENCY LEADERSHIP THEORY

About a decade after Hersey and Blanchard presented the situational leadership theory, the *contingency leadership theory* was developed. This theory is also related to what the literature refers to as "leader-match theory" (Fiedler & Chemers, 1984), where leaders are matched to differing situations. So, we are basically talking about a match between a leader's style and various situations.

Fiedler suggests that a leader's style is either task motivated or relationship motivated. Task-motivated leaders deal mostly with goal setting and accomplishment, while relationship-motivated leaders concentrate more on closer interpersonal relationships with employees. These styles will fit nicely into our Figure 2.1 and are more geared toward management and leadership behaviors.

Fiedler was the first to specifically categorize situational variables: (1) leader-member relations, (2) task structure, and (3) position power. Leader-member relations involve the confidence and loyalty workers have for their leader. Leaders with appropriate task structure are very clear and specific when relating goals and objectives to members of the organization. Position power is simply the amount of authority a leader has in making decisions.

## Path-Goal Theory of Leadership

In the early 1970s, House and Dressler (House, 1971; House & Dressler, 1974) popularized the *path-goal theory*. This theory focuses on what motivates members of the organization to perform well, and whether or not they feel appropriately rewarded for their work. So the challenge for the leader is to implement a leadership style that best meets the motivational needs of the worker.

House and Dressler suggest that effective leadership requires making the "path to the goal" clear to all in the organization, and involves (a) appropriate coaching, (b) removal of the obstacles that make reaching the goal difficult, and (c) making work satisfying to all.

Within the path-goal theory are four distinct styles of leadership: (1) directive leadership, (2) supportive leadership, (3) participatory leadership, and (4) achievement-oriented leadership. We could easily add the components of the path-goal theory to our Figure 2.1.

It is interesting to note that the path-goal theory is the first model to address the issue of motivation. It is also the first theory to come along that begins to address "practicality," and points to the real purpose of leadership being to guide and coach members of the organization toward the achievement of goals and objectives.

## TRANSFORMATIONAL LEADERSHIP THEORY

*Transformational leadership theory* surfaced quite recently and is credited to the work of James MacGregor Burns (1978). Burns presents two types of leadership: *transactional* and *transformational*. He considers most of the previous models presented in this chapter to be transactional, in that they focus on what happens between leaders and their followers. Principals who offer bonuses to teachers who successfully raise student test scores exhibit transactional leadership. Teachers who routinely give students a grade for work completed are practicing transactional leadership. In both of these examples, the "exchange" between the leader and follower is quite simple: You do this, and I will give you that.

Leaders who practice transformational leadership, on the other hand, pay special attention to the needs and desires of the followers and try to help members achieve their highest potential. Basically, the theme is to give more attention to the follower's needs than the leader's needs. Transformational leaders often exhibit strong values and ideals and can motivate people to act in ways that support the organization above their own self-interests (Kuhnert, 1994). Please see Figure 2.2.

## A CONCEPTUAL FRAMEWORK FOR
## LEADING FROM BELOW THE SURFACE

The leaders I will begin to describe (below the surface) do not fit into any of the formal leadership theories presented in this

**Figure 2.2**  Management and Leadership Behavior

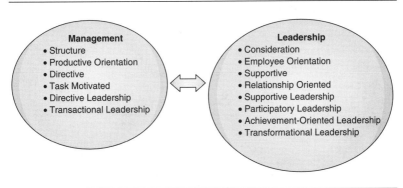

chapter. Many of the individual traits and behaviors described in these theories are evident. But I contend that truly effective school leaders possess and passionately pursue a third group of traits/behaviors, and it is these that form the titles of the chapters in this book.

One of the purposes of presenting the historical look at leadership over the last half century is to demonstrate that *leading from below the surface* is not so much a theory in itself, but rather a product of the progression of leadership theory. Its time has come. Just as the work of the Ohio and Michigan studies in the 1960s and 1970s drew attention to the differences between structure and consideration, we have progressed to a point that we now realize the difference between and value of such things as (a) evidence-based decision making, (b) collaboration as opposed to cooperation, (c) the importance of strategy, and (d) looking beyond the obvious. Figure 2.3 displays the framework that helps us with our further discussion of leading from below the surface.

School leaders can certainly benefit from the work of Stoghill, Hersey and Blanchard, Fiedler, House, and MacGregor Burns. But the quiet, less visible, non-charismatic leaders I discuss in these pages really spend more time and effort in the third area displayed in Figure 2.3. We will investigate these leadership qualities in the chapters ahead. But first, I will address in more specifics and detail the true meaning of leading from below the surface in the following chapter.

**Figure 2.3**    Theoretical Framework for
Leading From Below the Surface

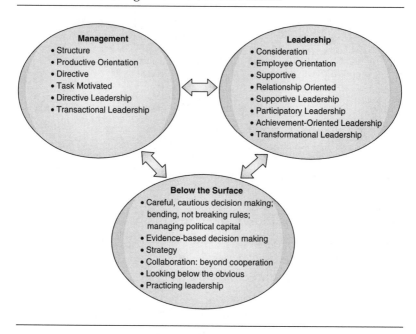

**Management**
- Structure
- Productive Orientation
- Directive
- Task Motivated
- Directive Leadership
- Transactional Leadership

**Leadership**
- Consideration
- Employee Orientation
- Supportive
- Relationship Oriented
- Supportive Leadership
- Participatory Leadership
- Achievement-Oriented Leadership
- Transformational Leadership

**Below the Surface**
- Careful, cautious decision making; bending, not breaking rules; managing political capital
- Evidence-based decision making
- Strategy
- Collaboration: beyond cooperation
- Looking below the obvious
- Practicing leadership

**Below the Surface**

- **Careful, cautious decision making; bending, not breaking rules; managing political capital**
- Evidence-based decision making
- Strategy
- Collaboration: beyond cooperation
- Looking below the obvious
- Practicing leadership

CHAPTER THREE

# What Is Leading From Below the Surface?

When we think of great effective leaders, names like John Kennedy, Golda Meir, Colin Powell, Margaret Thatcher, and Martin Luther King may come to mind. In education, we all can think of a few nationally known figures who are credited with strong educational leadership. Some lead our large urban districts (e.g., former Colorado Governor Roy Romer in Los Angeles) and still others are recognized as national policy makers (e.g., Secretary of Education Rod Paige). Certainly a few former U.S. secretaries of education should join this prestigious list, such as Diane Ravitch and William Bennett. These truly great educational leaders can be counted on one hand, but what of the majority of men and women leading our schools today? When looking closely, we realize that today's effective principals and superintendents do not fit the stereotype of *courageous, risk-taking, charismatic, and dynamic* individuals. In fact, the effective school principal is not highly visible, is not nationally recognized, charismatic, or necessarily out in front of the organization. Don't misunderstand me—some are, and they are truly valued in our educational arena. But many of our effective principals are modest and unassuming. They may not be charismatic, but they effectively lead schools in a quiet and low-key manner. What does this low-key, quiet leader look like?

Badaracco (2002), in his unorthodox guide to effective leadership, *Leading Quietly*, points to the great Albert Schweitzer as a person who changed many lives and inspired countless others. Schweitzer wrote these words in his autobiography, addressing the role of great individuals reshaping the world:

> Of all the will toward the ideal in mankind, only a small part can manifest itself in public action. All the rest of this force must be content with small and obscure deeds. The sum of these, however, is a thousand times stronger than the acts of those who receive wide public recognition. The latter, compared to the former, are like foam on the waves of a deep ocean. (Schweitzer, 1963, p. 74)

Badaracco goes on to state,

> Here is Albert Schweitzer, a great man, telling us to rethink and even devalue the role of great figures in human affairs. Schweitzer compares their efforts to the "foam" and instead praises "small and obscure deeds." (p. 3)

If we reexamine leadership, and especially the work of effective principals in our schools, we see men and women who are distant from the much-praised description of effective leadership in much of the present literature. They are *not* highly visible, charismatic, visionary, or out in the front of the charge. But they *are* effectively leading schools, dedicated to improved teaching and student learning, and having a positive impact on educational improvement and reform.

There is a general absence in the present leadership literature of what really sets leaders from below the surface apart from the more traditional courageous, charismatic principal. In Badaracco's research, he found a number of characteristics that set these leaders apart, and these qualities have more to do with character than tactics. "These men and women relied heavily on three unglamorous virtues: restraint, modesty, and tenacity" (2002, p. 170).

Principals who lead from below the surface actually consider some of our more traditional and accepted forms of leadership a danger. Much of our leadership preparation and training focuses on (a) making decisions quickly and aggressively, (b) thinking across the whole organization as we consider problems and decisions, and (c) considering all decisions to be both important and urgent. For example, a popular leadership theorist suggests that we change the metaphor of "ready, aim, fire" to "ready, fire, aim." It seems to me that this suggestion encourages quick, rapid decision making. In addition, I am not convinced that we all believe some issues are more important than others and that some are urgent and some are not, but when observing and talking with practicing principals, they tell us that a distinction between importance and urgency is not often made in their daily work of leading schools. Perhaps the correct metaphor is "ready, aim, aim, aim, aim, fire."

My work with school principals and superintendents has uncovered the same conclusions as we read in Badaracco's work. Principals who lead from below the surface actually consider the three points above to be dangers to effective leadership. The following are descriptions of how those who lead from below the surface address these dangers:

1. Principals who lead from below the surface must be careful of quick decisions and proceeding at a lightning speed.

2. Principals who lead from below the surface don't set out to prove anything or solve the world's problems: They operate slowly, carefully, cautiously, and really just want to do their small part in the grand scheme of things.

3. Principals who lead from below the surface have the ability to distinguish between importance and urgency. These principals are masters at picking their causes—causes that they care about deeply and see through to the end.

## BENDING THE RULES WITHOUT BREAKING THEM

I am not aware of any of the current literature on school leadership associating bending the rules with responsible school leadership. We're taught to not stray from the rules and to follow closely the rules, policies, and guidelines set forth by the school board. But many times, situations before us are more complicated and exist below the surface in a gray area of ambiguity.

Many of you have undoubtedly had experience with interpreting and perhaps even creating school district policy. As important as a strict set of rules is for effective leadership in schools, it is not a stretch to say that it is almost impossible to create a set of rules that cover all the different situations encountered in a school day. Schools are very complex, with a variety of ever-changing dilemmas that do not always lend themselves to a specific rule for solution. Principals often find themselves in specific situations in which the rules do not apply, and encounter others where following the rules is a mistake and can actually cause further problems. For example, several years ago, as a superintendent of a small rural school district in California, I found myself faced with the decision of whether or not to hire the wife of the current principal. She was clearly the top choice of the selection committee, and I could personally attest to her fine teaching, expertise in content area, and exemplary service in a neighboring district. However, the district policy was very clear: The district shall not employ a teacher who is a direct relative of the supervising administrator. In this case, the principal would be the evaluator of the prospective candidate—his wife.

First of all, please do not misinterpret my message here: I am suggesting that occasionally rules need a *bending,* not necessarily a *breaking.* I was reluctant, for a variety of reasons, to break the rule. But I struggled with obeying the rule mechanically and perhaps causing further harm and hard feelings with personnel. Leading from below the surface involves looking for ways to creatively and imaginatively bend the rules without breaking them. With the help of members of the school board, and a revisit to board policy, we together decided to hire the principal's wife, but assign her evaluation to another principal at the high school. As you see, we did not break or change the rule: We bent the rule by providing another supervising administrator.

When facing complex ethical dilemmas, leading from below the surface requires following two guidelines advised by Badaracco: (1) take the rules very seriously, and (2) look creatively and imaginatively for ways to follow the spirit of the rules while, at the same time, bending them (2002, p. 218). Ubben and Hughes (2000), in their highly regarded text entitled *The Principal: Creative Leadership for Effective Schools*, discuss "creative insubordination" and suggest that good leaders seem to know when it is more important to "beg forgiveness" than to "ask permission" (p. 8). Some have called this discretionary disobedience. Whatever one calls it, the behavior does seem to be common among all effective school leaders.

## MANAGING YOUR PORTFOLIO OF POLITICAL CAPITAL

Much of the leadership literature emphasizes the importance of political acumen in effective school leadership. Cuban (2001) used the word *political* to "represent the means of getting done what needs to be done in an unpredictable, uncertain world" (p. 107). Ubben and Hughes (2000) further state, "There are situations where principals use both formal and informal influences to persuade, deflect, and use any resources at hand—students, teachers, parents, other school administrators—to build support for a desirable outcome or to overcome opposition to such an outcome" (p. 8).

The current yo-yo performance of the stock market gives me an appropriate analogy here. Leading from below the surface requires that before getting involved in risky situations, you always check to see how much political capital you have. This elusive characteristic consists mainly of your reputation and relationship with the school community. In a sense, your political capital consists mostly of perceptions in the minds of other people. As we lead from below the surface to take action on a critical issue, we always pay close attention to how much political capital we have and how much we are risking, and just as important, we consider the likely returns on our investment.

In other words, effective school leaders must act like venture capitalists: We must be willing to take significant risks, but only if there seems to be a prospect of making a significant difference. If things go well, we consider investing more heavily; if not, we try to reduce the risks.

The hiring of the principal's wife, though only bending the rule and approved by the board, carried a risk. On one hand, the board, parents, and other community members supported the hiring of the candidate, but on the other hand, there was a risk of dissatisfaction among the teaching staff who questioned the bending of the rule and the practice of nepotism. Checking my political capital, I decided the investment to be a wise one, but not without some risk. Did I see a return on my investment? Not quickly, but eventually, yes.

## BOURDIEU AND CAPITAL

The work of Pierre Bourdieu (1990) presents the notion of *capital* as a "generalized resource that can assume monetary and non-monetary as well as tangible and intangible forms" (p. 122). Capital takes time to accumulate, and its potential capacity to produce "profits" is governed by conditions within a person's particular social world and can have unequal distributions (Bourdieu, 1986, as cited in Paso, 2003). The point to be made here is that a school leader does not *begin* with political capital; it must be accumulated over time. Once accumulated, one must be in control of its distribution.

Political capital is mostly formed by one's reputation and relationship with others (faculty, staff, students, parents, and business and community leaders). Let me close this chapter with a final example of accumulated political capital. In my opening introduction in Chapter 1, I shared my experience of building reconstruction while serving as superintendent of a small rural school district in California. There is more to that story, related to political capital.

After evaluating the limited amount of state reconstruction allocation funds we were to receive, we decided to place an additional bond on the ballot for voter consideration. This bond, if approved, would allow us to completely and thoroughly address the needs of our somewhat dilapidated building and grounds. The task before us was to convince the taxpayers in our district that the bond funds were truly needed. The board charged me with this task.

I decided that I was going to personally contact each and every registered voter in our district. Time consuming? Yes, it took approximately one year. But I managed to contact every person listed on the election board's records. In addition, I tried to increase my political capital further by contacting non-registered voters (of which small rural districts in the agricultural belt have many) and provided voting registration materials for them.

My only goal was to garner support for the bond. But to my surprise, something additional occurred. I talked with some property owners who had never been approached or even communicated with by our school district personnel: They essentially were not aware of our district's existence. Soon, we had wealthy ranch owners contacting us at school to offer free use of heavy equipment and manpower (e.g., backhoes, bulldozers, and dump trucks). The local nursery owner wanted to donate all of the trees and shrubbery needed after construction was finished. I was invited by numerous groups (e.g., Rotary Club, Lion's Club, local bankers, etc.) to speak on the importance of building reconstruction and the passage of the bond. My political capital was increasing on several fronts.

There is no need to go on here, but I will share with you the outcome of our bond election: an unprecedented approval of 99%. This was a record approval in the state, a record that I think still stands today.

Even after we finished reconstruction, our landscaping, and new athletic facilities, much of the political capital I had been fortunate to secure stayed with me for years to come. I tried my best to invest it wisely, to watch my risks, and as important, to consider the likely returns on my investments.

CHAPTER FOUR

# *Evidence-Based Decision Making*

It is my belief that our students with special needs (limited-English speaking, students of color, students with disabilities) are "below the surface." On and above the clearly visible surface are the majority of our students: the average and above-average. But getting to the needs of our special populations requires leaders to "investigate and practice" effective strategies that take us below the visible surface.

It is no exaggeration to state that our politicians and legislators are obsessed with the accountability of schools and especially obsessed with the ways we measure success. The very recent federal legislation, No Child Left Behind (U.S. Department of Education, 2001) requires that we focus more attention on "previously marginalized students." Though our many critics argue that education has failed these students, I contend that many of our principals and superintendents do an admirable job of providing high-quality instruction to all students. In doing so, they regularly and intentionally look below the surface for factors and phenomena causing any disparity in the teaching and learning domains.

Think of any current dialogue or discussion of education: Has accountability ever been mentioned *without* the inclusion of the word *testing?* Though some might argue that the words *accountability* and *testing* should not be used interchangeably, without question testing serves as the centerpiece of many, if not most, accountability systems (Waite, Boone, & McGhee, 2001, p. 184). It is beyond the scope of this book to discuss in detail the pros and cons of using tests to hold schools (and ultimately principals) accountable for student success. But suffice it to say, little research exists addressing the merits of tests and their appropriate applications (American Educational Research Association, 2001). This is the very critical reason why successful leaders *must* look below the surface to ensure that all students receive fair, equitable, rigorous, and appropriate instruction in our schools.

## BELOW THE SURFACE: DATA- OR EVIDENCE-BASED?

As I state repeatedly in this book, a critical component of leading from below the surface is a principal's practice (and willingness) to investigate below the existing data. To further emphasize my point, I want to share the results of a study conducted earlier in my career as a teacher for the Los Angeles Unified School District. This study is presented in greater detail in *Schools and Data: The Educator's Guide to Using Data to Improve Decision Making* (Creighton, 2001), but a brief overview here will provide another example of leading from below the surface and emphasize the importance of reaching below existing data.

When I was working as a sixth-grade teacher for the Los Angeles Unified School District in the early 1980s, the Los Angeles Police Department implemented the now-famous and nationally recognized D.A.R.E. program. As you probably know, the program's purpose is to educate students about the dangers of drugs, alcohol, tobacco, and gang violence.

As teachers, we were pretty convinced that students' attitudes toward drugs and alcohol changed for the better during their sixth-grade year when they were involved in the D.A.R.E. program. The *existing data* showed a positive effect on our students' attitudes. But our real question and concern was: Did students begin to revert back to their negative attitudes as they moved up into the junior-high grades?

We administered a student attitudinal survey to a fifth-grade class to get an idea of their attitudes before D.A.R.E. involvement. We administered a similar survey to the same class in sixth grade after they completed the D.A.R.E. training. Finally, we administered the attitudinal survey to the same group of students after the completion of seventh grade—a full year after receiving D.A.R.E. training.

The results may not be that surprising: Scores noticeably went from low in fifth grade, to medium/high in sixth grade, only to fall back down significantly in seventh grade. Here is where many folks might stop and interpret the existing data without investigating further, below the surface.

We need to be careful that we do not create a *cause and effect* interpretation here. Some might argue that D.A.R.E. causes negative attitudes regarding drugs because the students' attitudes declined after the first year. No, not necessarily! Perhaps the results are due to other societal factors (junior-high school environment, the transition from elementary school to junior high, etc.) that caused this change in attitudes.

The finding does not indicate that the program is ineffective, but it does indicate to us that the efforts must continue for more than 1 year. Since that time, the program has been expanded down to fifth grade and up through seventh grade. I suspect the reason for this expansion is related to our earlier findings. Also, the contact time with the D.A.R.E. officer consists of 1 or 2 hours per week. We suspected that this short amount of time produced short-term attitudinal effects. So you see, the "culprit" may not be the D.A.R.E. program itself but the extremely limited amount of time spent on activities and instruction.

My point is that with the heavy emphasis on principals making data-based decisions, and the unending pressure from the state and federal governments for accountability, there is a tendency to just look at existing data. I can think of no situation that does not benefit from a much deeper and thorough investigation. The most recent findings related to student dropout rates in our larger urban cities (e.g., New York, Chicago, Houston, Los Angeles) are a case in point. Existing data indicate rates in the range of 2%–8%, but school leaders willing and committed to investigating below the surface find that rates really approximate 25%–50%. In addition, we suspect large numbers are actually "pushed out" by our school districts and administrators. This is a very complex issue and beyond the scope of this book to settle. But suffice it to say, we desperately need principals and other school leaders who are willing to "look below the tip of the iceberg."

## DATA-DRIVEN VS. EVIDENCE-BASED DECISION MAKING

The following examples help differentiate between these two terms. Data-based decision making is the current buzz term in education circles today. We have entire courses in our preparation programs devoted to the use of data to improve decision making in our schools. This author himself has spent considerable time and effort on the subject (*Schools and Data,* Creighton, 2001). To help make the point that perhaps we have gone astray with this emphasis on data, let me provide a couple of examples.

Many of my examples come from the Houston Independent School District. Part of the reason for this is the fact that I currently work for Sam Houston State University, an hour's drive north of Houston. In addition, the students who enroll in our Masters and Doctoral Programs come from the Houston and North Houston area schools. But beyond these reasons, another is somewhat significant. In Linda McNeil's powerfully written *Contradictions of School Reform* (2000), she states in the author's preface,

The setting for this book is Houston, Texas. This is extremely significant. Houston has the fifth largest public school system in the United States. More than 150 home languages are spoken by the children in its public schools. For a simple and powerful reason, what happens in

Houston can quickly affect the entire nation: Texas is the second largest state in the United States, and its political power increasingly sets the national agenda. (p. xxi)

Leaders come from all corners. Though Linda McNeil is a professor at Rice University, I consider her to be one of the great educators who "leads from below the surface." I will return later to an example of her research and work that will again demonstrate a distinction between data-based decision making and evidence-based decision making.

## ATTENDANCE RATES VS. ABSENCE RATES

You are most likely familiar with the term *average daily attendance* (ADA). We collect these data for several reasons, but primarily to determine the number of dollars we receive in state and federal monies. Simply put, if students are present, we receive additional funding to help educate them. In addition, schools are given accountability ratings based upon ADA. So principals and superintendents give heavy emphasis to implementing strategies that keep attendance rates high.

Many of the schools receiving the highest accountability rating (Exemplary) report ADA in a range of 92%–98%. A 92% sounds pretty good and even has a connotation of a grade of A, right? So we, as school administrators, report that on average, we have 92% of our students in attendance.

John Barrera, a principal at Las Americas School in Houston, is a leader who looks below the surface and asks a different question, one perhaps not so much related to state funding, but certainly related to quality instruction. If the ADA is 92%, what about the absence rate? That's simple—8%. So John brings a different question to the surface: On average, how many of our students are absent? Investigating a little further below the surface, John comes up with the following important issue related to "evidence-based" decision making.

If, on average, 8% of the students are absent, and based on a year of 180 days of instruction, these students are missing approximately 2 weeks of school per year (2% of 180 equals 14.4 days). John concludes that his school's Exemplary Rating based on a 92% attendance rate is one thing, but students missing two weeks of school per year is quite another. You may argue that focusing on attendance is no different than focusing on absence. Well, it is all a matter of perspective, and reflects a characteristic of those who lead from below the surface. John cares deeply for the marginal students, and he believes that looking at the absence rate rather than the attendance rate gives him a better chance of focusing on students at risk of educational failure. Yes, he concerns himself with data, but digs deeper for further *evidence* to more effectively lead his school.

## NARROWING THE ACHIEVEMENT GAP

Here is another example where making decisions simply based on existing data does not work for the benefit of students at risk of educational failure. Again we turn to the Houston Independent School District, but I suggest this could (and perhaps does) happen in any school district across the nation.

During the 2000 Presidential Debates (Commission on Presidential Debates, 2000), George Bush and Al Gore tossed much rhetoric back and forth related to school accountability and student-testing programs. The argument continued to focus on whether the Clinton Administration or the state of Texas had a better understanding of accountability. Governor Bush (now President Bush) was (and still is) fond of pointing to the "narrowing of student achievement gaps" in the state of Texas. The same claim was presented by Rod Paige (then Superintendent of Houston School District) and continues to be heard from the current Secretary of Education. Figure 4.1 displays data we often saw referred to by both politicians.

Sure enough! The data reported were basically correct and accurate. But certain area superintendents and principals began to investigate below the surface. The data in Figure 4.1 represent test scores of students tested. OK, this sounds like a "no brainer," but wait a minute! Who were the students *not*

**Figure 4.1**    Narrowing the Achievement Gap

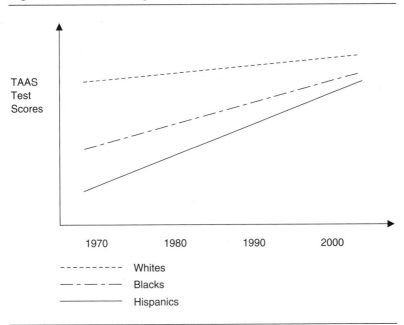

being tested? In other words, let's look closely at the students represented (and not represented). The answers to this question illustrate the danger in making decisions on existing data only.

It turns out that approximately 28% of the African-American and Hispanic students had dropped out between the time they enrolled in school and the time these tests were administered. Paralleling this important evidence, in a national study, Haney (1999) found that only 50% of African-American and Hispanic students enrolled in our nation's public schools have actually progressed to high school graduation. Is it unreasonable to assume that this large number of minority students dropping out of school was eliminated and not included in the testing pool reported in Figure 4.1, and if they were not in the testing pool, that the academic performance (test scores) of these particular groups would likely rise? We are assuming, of course, that these minority groups would likely represent lower scores in the testing pool.

Looking below the surface further, our principals found other factors that might have accounted for this "narrowing of the gap" in student achievement. The number of students identified as special education students, and thus qualified for exemption from taking these reported standardized tests, nearly doubled between 1994 and 1998. This finding also seems likely to have narrowed the gap only on the surface. Most alarming is an additional finding by Haney (2000) that reports only 70% of students in Texas actually graduated from school in the 1990s—a "below-the-surface" missing-student rate of 30%, or approximately 700,000 children. I am not questioning the increase in special education students or the importance of providing services to them; I am only pointing to the importance of including *all the evidence* that lies below the surface that is required in addition to data when making wise educational decisions.

I also repeat my finding in looking at effective school leaders, that many are more concerned with the "below-the-surface" characteristics displayed in the conceptual framework we looked at in Figure 2.3. As did John Barrera in our earlier example, a few principals now are focusing more on the missing students and reasons for their absence than they are on the claims of politicians who tout huge gains in test scores and the narrowing of the achievement gap.

As I am currently writing this chapter, a few courageous leaders in the Houston School District have looked below the surface and uncovered evidence indicating that school and district administrators have actually held students back a grade to prevent them from entering the testing pool. In other words, testing currently takes place in tenth grade: Some students who are not expected to do well on the state standardized test are temporarily held as ninth graders, thus keeping them from the testing pool. In essence, what happens here is that this particular group of students bypasses the taking of the test altogether. They are held back while the test takes place, then promoted before the next test-taking date. Isn't there an ethical issue here?

## Dropout Rate: 2% or 28%?

Over the past few years, the Houston School District has reported unusually low percentages of student dropouts in the district. City and state reports reveal an impressive 1%–2% dropout rate for Whites, and an equally impressive 2%–3% for Blacks, Hispanics, and other minority populations. In addition, the state of Texas designated the Houston district as above average or "Exemplary" in its Academic Excellence Indicator System (AEIS). This rating is based on several factors, one of which is low student dropout rates. Another factor is the student achievement of minority groups, drawing more attention to the evidence I presented above related to the narrowing of the gap.

In the summer of 2003, the Houston School District was recognized as the outstanding urban school district in the nation by the Eli Broad Foundation, partially based on the reported narrowing of the achievement gap and the low dropout rates. However, recent evidence has surfaced indicating that the district may have falsely reported dropout data. Daily reports in the *Houston Chronicle* point to poor record keeping and some falsification of data at various schools in the district. Actual dropout rates seem to be closer to 20%–30% for minority populations. As I write this chapter (July 2003), review teams from the Texas Education Agency (TEA) are investigating this further and are contemplating changing the "exemplary" rating to one of "below average."

I return for a moment to Joseph Badaracco (2002) and his popular book, *Leading Quietly*.

If we look at leadership with a wide-angle lens, we can see men and women who are far from heroes and people from the top of organizations, but are yet solving important problems and contributing to a better world. (p. 5)

The vast majority of difficult, human problems—both inside and outside organizations—are not solved by a swift, decisive stroke from someone at the top. What usually matters are careful, thoughtful, small, practical efforts by people working far from the limelight. In short, quiet leadership is what moves and changes the world. (p. 9)

Somewhere, below the surface and out of the limelight, leaders are challenging the Houston School District's claims of narrowing achievement gaps and low dropout rates. Though they are not yet identified or highly visible, I suspect these leaders are building-level principals, teachers, and attendance clerks, guided by a willingness and commitment to look below the surface in the name of social justice, equity, and fairness for all children, especially those at risk of educational failure.

## CONCLUDING THOUGHTS

The Assessment Committee of the President's Advisory Committee on Educational Excellence for Hispanic Americans (2000) reported that more than 2 million Hispanic students have been underrepresented or ignored because they may have been excluded from state testing programs. Critics have also reported that the pressure on low-achieving and minority students has been so intense that it has caused many of them to drop out of school (McNeil, 2000).

I believe we are currently at a fork in the road. If we continue to focus mostly on the surface, huge numbers of minority and at-risk students will continue to fall farther and farther behind and worse, out of the learning organization altogether. On the other hand, if we can learn and practice "below-the-surface strategies," our education system has a chance to choose the right road. As someone once said, "Leadership cannot be learned; leadership *is* learning."

**Below the Surface**

- Careful, cautious decision making; bending, not breaking rules; managing political capital
- Evidence-based decision making
- **Strategy**
- Collaboration: beyond cooperation
- Looking below the obvious
- Practicing leadership

CHAPTER FIVE

# *Institutional Effectiveness vs. Strategy*

The accountability movement has certainly been responsible for school leaders focusing on program and organizational effectiveness. The demand for higher teacher and student performance requires principals to spend much time on developing strategies such as site-based management, organizational learning communities, total quality management, curriculum mapping, test-taking skills, accelerated reading programs, and so on. All of these strategies are pursued to increase institutional effectiveness. It is too commonplace for principals, superintendents, communities, and legislators to equate high test scores with institutional effectiveness.

But principals and superintendents who lead from below the surface reach beyond that and practice "strategy." Strategy is needed to address such issues as dropout rates, attendance, and students who are at risk of educational failure. Let me provide an example of a district's leadership concentrating on institutional effectiveness, but failing to address strategy, by returning to a previous discussion of the Houston Independent School District (ISD).

The Houston ISD's recognition by the Eli Broad Foundation and their state accountability exemplary rating are certainly signs of institutional effectiveness. However, as we noted in the previous chapter, evidence surfaced indicating that the district may have falsely reported dropout data. *Houston Chronicle* daily reports revealed poor recordkeeping and actual dropout rates close to 20%–30% for minority populations.

The superintendent and board were faced with finding a quick explanation. "We are looking into the problem," stated the superintendent. It was immediately obvious that the district had no "strategy" in place, or even in the wings, to address the dropout problem. The district continues to side-step the issue even today.

Part of the problem is the district's failure to distinguish between institutional effectiveness and strategy. An over-emphasis on test scores, AEIS accountability ratings, and national awards from outside philanthropists (Eli Broad Foundation) certainly contributed to institutional effectiveness, but when sudden trouble hit, a strategy was needed quickly. The necessary blend of institutional effectiveness and strategy may be analogous to what we have come to call management and leadership skills. A leader certainly needs to know how to manage—keeping the buses on time and the budgets balanced. But leading from below the surface also requires instructional leadership—focusing on the achievement of all students, creativity, and problem solving.

School leaders who only emphasize institutional effectiveness concern themselves with performing similar and common goals. But leaders who add strategy begin to consider different ways of accomplishing the same (and additional) goals. Institutional effectiveness and strategy are both necessary components of effective school leadership. But they are different, and leaders who only concentrate on effectiveness without strategy run the risk of static organizations, perpetuating the status quo.

## A Closer Look at Strategy

Let's look at how Michael Porter (1996), one of the world's most influential thinkers on business organization, defines strategy. Though his definition applies to economics and business, I suggest it is equally applicable to effective school leadership.

> Strategy is about being different. It means deliberately choosing a set of activities to develop a unique mix of values. The need for strategy arises when there are groups with different needs and when a tailored set of activities can serve their needs best. (p. 45)

He continues,

> The challenge of developing or re-establishing a clear strategy is often primarily an organizational one and depends on leadership. Strong leaders willing to make choices are essential. (p. 70)

To practice strategy, school leaders work on multiple dimensions at the same time. For example, during our work with improving teacher and student performance, to truly accomplish these tasks we must also be aware of and address many different kinds of students (e.g., limited-English speakers, students with disabilities, and those who are at risk of educational failure). We want to have strategies for helping students who are at risk; we want to have strategies for helping limited-English speakers; and we want to have strategies for equalizing instruction for all of our students—No exceptions!

In many districts, school leadership is limited to satisfying the requirements of state department regulations and policies, an overemphasis on test scores at the expense of providing the rich curriculum we know students deserve, and a focus on *institutional effectiveness*. It is interesting to note here that institutional effectiveness is generally defined by those furthest from our schools and students (i.e., politicians and policy makers). But the leader's role (and responsibility) is much broader and comprehensive. School leadership is more than the characteristics espoused by university preparation programs and state and national standards. I agree with Michael Porter: The core of leadership is strategy—looking deeper and more broadly at issues and students who are not visible in the frame of institutional effectiveness.

## How Does Strategy Relate to School Leadership?

First of all, let's make a distinction between strategic planning and strategy. Too often, we involve ourselves with strategic planning *after* we encounter a problem and want to develop a plan for improvement. For example, the superintendent calls and says we have a problem with low math and reading scores in the middle grades. So we embark on a strategic plan to improve student achievement.

Strategy, as I use the term in this book, is something school leaders do *before* a problem arises. It is almost as if we are putting a plan together for the "what if" or "if-then" scenario. Critical is the realization that a school can engage in strategic planning—but lack strategy. Strategic planning most often deals with the more visible and obvious; strategy deals with the less obvious and not always visible or tangible.

Strategy in its simplest form is in place for our school fire drills. We develop a strategy for the possibility of "what if" or "if-then." If a fire breaks out, then we have a strategy for evacuating the building ASAP for the safety of our students and staff.

During my teaching days with the Los Angeles Unified School District, I was impressed with my principal's decision to put a strategy in place in the event of an earthquake. As you know, the strategy required for an earthquake drill is different than a strategy for a fire drill: evaluation of students and staff is not a desirable or recommended component in case of earthquakes. Children and teachers are safer staying in their classrooms and taking cover.

A critical component of my principal's strategy really took place later. After the all-clear directive, we quickly took our students to the playground and parking lot, as far from the building as possible. In teams of two, teachers and staff were assigned a certain section of the building to inspect for damage or missing children (e.g., the kindergarten wing). My assignment, with my partner, was four second-grade classrooms on the third floor of the building. Even though this strategy was merely a drill, it was designed to simulate reality: on occasion, we would find a student in a corner with a sign around her neck saying, "Student with cut forehead from flying window glass." The principal always secretively placed 4 to 6 students in various locations serving as "pretend casualties." My partner and I were faced with decisions such as, Do we apply a bandage? Do we carry the student to the nurse's office? Do we call for a stretcher? We all felt pretty sure that the strategy for earthquakes was a good one—and in the best interest of student safety.

In the years to follow, as my career took me to other districts, I encountered the *strategy* for foggy days in Fresno, California. The superintendent had a strategy in place in the event that our buses could not drive safely to pick our students up in the morning. In addition, all teachers and staff were required to take CPR and first aid classes on an annual basis to ready us for unexpected accidents in the classroom or on the playground.

I consider all of the previously mentioned examples of strategy to be on-the-surface strategies, focused on the obvious: building fires occur, earthquakes in L.A. are frequent, and foggy days in Fresno are certain.

As volatile as our present educational environment is, and as likely as it is that leading our schools will continue to become more complex, attention to below-the-surface strategy is critical. Who among us would have thought a decade ago that we would need a strategy for a Columbine? Who among us would have devised a strategy for coping with gang-related happenings in our schools? But again, even these more recent examples of strategy center around tragedy; tragedy forces us to develop and implement strategies. Let's explore for a moment strategy for leading from below the surface, in ways that are not so visible or obvious.

Presently, I am very troubled about something stated by our current Secretary of Education, Rod Paige. In a speech to a National Press Club meeting, he warned of an unrecognized educational crisis of disadvantaged students who he says are written off at our schools and unready for a complex world. He cited discouraging statistics about the performance of Blacks and Hispanics on reading and math tests in high school and on college-entrance exams. He went on to say,

> Those who are unprepared will sit on the sidelines, confronting poverty, dead-end jobs, and hopelessness. They will find little choice and much despair. The well-educated will live in a world of their own choosing; the poorly educated will wander in the shadows. The majority of students falling behind are poor, and effectively, the education circumstances of these students are not unlike a system of apartheid. ("Secretary Paige Suggests Apartheid," 2003)

Wow! Pretty sharp words, huh? I would respond, though, that we have done much already to address this issue. Many of our schools are the finest in the world, and our school leaders are very aware and sensitive to this problem. I would also argue that our congress and president have failed to provide the necessary monies that states and schools need to carry out the mission of the law (No Child Left Behind). But more relevant to the subject of this chapter, I do not feel we as educational leaders have appropriate strategies in place to address this problem in substantive ways. I want to use this example to walk through the process of establishing strategy in this below-the-surface issue. Stay with me on this one, as I borrow an organizational behavior theory to help us develop a potentially effective strategy for improving the education of our minority children.

Kurt Lewin (1951), a well-known researcher and writer in the development of several organizational behavior theories, came up with a model that I find helpful in designing strategy. He developed *force field analysis* as a model for identifying some of the factors that push for change and those that push against it. This model can help us set up a strategy for improving how we educate minority children. Force field analysis involves three components or steps:

1.  Describing the strategy and who and what it affects

2.  Identifying the forces that will support the strategy

3.  Identifying the forces that resist or oppose the strategy

Let's begin tackling number one above by describing the strategy.

## DESCRIBING THE STRATEGY

After a thorough investigation (evidence based) of the student subgroups enrolled in our advanced math classes, we find that very few Black and Hispanic students take these classes. So we are particularly interested in developing a strategy to increase opportunity and enrollment. We have decided to concentrate first on the base course, Pre-Algebra, assuming that minority students will then be more prepared for and interested in additional advanced classes. To accomplish this first step, we will need to hire a minimum of one new teacher, and perhaps two, depending on whether we will need to add one or two sections (associated cost: $40,000–$80,000). To gain support for this new program, we will have to conduct staff orientation meetings to inform the entire high school faculty of our plans. This will mostly involve time, but likely will require some monetary support ($5,000). The new classroom will need a minimum of three computers (and peripheral equipment) for technology-enhanced instruction ($3,000–$5,000). More time will be necessary to hold parent advisory meetings, board presentations, and individual advising of students to make sure all who will be affected by the program are considered.

This description perhaps isn't as complete as it could be. Much care should be taken to describe the strategy as thoroughly as possible, making sure that all individuals are consulted and informed, their needs and interests considered, and input encouraged and taken seriously. Let's now move to the next step: identifying forces that will affect the strategy.

## IDENTIFYING POSITIVE AND NEGATIVE FORCES

After the creation of a thorough description of the strategy, the strategists (principals) compile two lists: one that identifies all the forces that are likely to support the strategy and another list that identifies the forces that will potentially resist the strategy. Here are a few ideas to consider:

1. The estimated cost of our proposed strategy is approximately $90,000, which includes salaries, equipment, and training.

2. A new classroom will have to be provided.

3. There may be resistance from present faculty who might view this strategy as an attempt to "dumb down the curriculum."

4. The initial reaction of the school board members may be either positive or negative, or a combination. Some board members may need to be won over to support the strategy.

5. It has been rumored that certain segments of our student body (e.g., White students) may view this strategy as "reverse discrimination" and resent the special attention given to our minority students.

Again, this list is incomplete, but the point is that we consider every possible individual and group that will be affected and have an interest in the new strategy. Now, from the above list, let's compile our lists of positive and negative forces.

**Table 5.1**    Force Field Analysis

| Positive Forces | Negative Forces |
| --- | --- |
| 1. Strong support from board | 1. High cost for salaries/classroom |
| 2. Algebra 1 and Algebra 2 teachers are very excited | 2. White students view as reverse discrimination |
| 3. Initial parent feedback—positive | 3. Some faculty may resist |
| 4. Counselors report 40 interested students | 4. Time needed for orientation/training |

From here, we would begin our meetings and orientations with faculty, parents, and board members. One of the purposes of these initial meetings is to clearly validate these forces. We may have misjudged or made incorrect assumptions. Perhaps the initial parent positive responses came from a limited few. In addition, stakeholders may surprise you with a solution of their own: Board members may quickly eliminate the high cost by allocating the necessary funds from the budget. This final step involves an attempt to increase the positive forces and reduce the negative forces. This takes time and should not be rushed. Getting the support of the board may be quick and easy. But identifying the possibility of faculty resistance may not surface as quickly. Assuming that the resistance does not exist because it does not surface right away is a serious mistake for the leader from below the surface.

I believe the Lewin model to be a useful tool for investigating, developing, and implementing strategy. There will always be resistance to strategies for new programs. Lewin's force field analysis can help us understand where the resistance comes from, what it represents, and the magnitude of the resistance. The process is hard and time consuming. However, my experience in observing principals who lead from below the surface reveals that they are not impatient or deterred by hard work; they actually seem to thrive on it.

Having differentiated in this chapter between institutional effectiveness and strategy, we now move on to another distinction in the next chapter: collaboration vs. cooperation. In a similar way, I suggest that principals and school leaders who lead from below the surface do not see these two activities or practices as the same.

**Below the Surface**

- Careful, cautious decision making; bending, not breaking rules; managing political capital
- Evidence-based decision making
- Strategy
- **Collaboration: beyond cooperation**
- Looking below the obvious
- Practicing leadership

CHAPTER SIX

# *Cooperation vs. Collaboration*

Though we may agree that leading from below the surface requires collaboration, let's be clear about its meaning. To do so, we need to draw upon the expertise of Dean Corregan, from the Texas A & M Department of Educational Administration. Corregan (2001) posits that there is a great deal of difference among collaboration, cooperation, and coordination. In particular, collaboration is a higher-level activity than either of the other two. He states,

> Individuals and groups can cooperate and coordinate without changing what they are doing. In collaboration however, the expectation is that the new collaboration entity produces something that individuals or organizations could not produce alone. Collaboration takes a long time; it cannot be developed overnight. It involves building trust and confidence, and that takes time. (p. 177)

To further help get at the meaning of collaboration, and how leading from below the surface accesses it, let's return for a moment to the work of William Isaacs (1999). In his discussion of the effective use of dialogue, he talks about the importance of *suspending.* When you enter into discussion with others, you have two choices: (1) defend your view while resisting the views of others or (2) suspend your opinion and certainties that lie behind it. Suspension means, "we neither suppress what we think, nor advocate it with unilateral conviction" (p. 134). Rather, we develop our thinking in a way that contributes to the creative energy of the entire group. If each person suspends his or her thinking in this way, the group begins to enter into a zone where the contribution of each member helps produce a greater whole. This experience creates something that individuals could not produce alone. Collaboration really means looking deeper below the surface of cooperating and coordinating.

Let's think for a moment about the typical parent advisory committee we commonly utilize in our schools. Most often, the school administrator opens the session with the announcement of a plan—let's say to raise funds for the new football stadium. The administrator announces his or her "certainties" about the importance of the stadium and the need to raise additional funding. In a sense, this idea has absolute certainty and necessity attached, and carries with it a *non-negotiability.* The decision has already been made—we will build a new football stadium. But wait a minute! Maybe that's not the problem. Maybe the parent advisory committee should have been called in sooner to determine if resources might be better utilized and implemented elsewhere. In this example, the administrator had his or her certainties in place—and to now ask the parent advisory committee for help with the project is only a façade, involving cooperation and coordination at best, without any real hope of collaboration.

In collaboration, the message is clear: No single school leader can assume the full responsibility for creating the conditions that will have the greatest impact on organizational effectiveness and student learning.

Let's revisit John Barrera, a Houston ISD principal who practices "below the surface leadership." Visiting John's school, Las Americas Learning Center, in Houston, one sees something very different occurring. One of John's many strengths is his successful efforts with community-based collaboration systems. His school partners include a wide variety of stakeholders: other schools, parents, community organizations (public and private service agencies), civic groups, businesses, and colleges and universities. John's school is an example of what Corregan (2001) refers to as "an interprofessional educational program" (p. 179), with simultaneous renewal occurring between the students and staff at Las Americas and the community organizations in partnership with the school.

The Task Force on Interprofessional Education (1995), which included representatives from 17 universities, summarized what its members had learned from developing interprofessional educational programs (in Corregan, 2001, pp. 181–182):

1. Learning occurs in multiple contexts.

2. Real experience is the best teaching method; simulation is OK; the didactic method is the worst. Espoused theory must be translated into theory in use.

3. Professional behavior must be driven by personal vision to enable children and families to deal with problems.

4. No one model for teaching collaborative behavior is desirable. A combination of models is desirable.

5. The learning process determines what will be learned.

6. Experiential learning develops bonding and advocacy.

7. Collaborative practice involves simultaneous renewal.

8. In trying to change the status quo, interprofessional education will confront many barriers.

9. Interprofessional collaboration must begin with individuals, requiring vision and respect for and understanding of colleagues.

10. Attitude and orientation are as important as skills and knowledge in promoting relationships rather than individual orientation.

11. Respect for social, ethnic, and professional differences is required of professionals who are working together.

12. Universities could be part of the answer, not part of the problem.

13. Leadership requires letting go and giving over; it involves creating conditions so others can succeed.

14. Involvement of all players in initial planning promotes development of ownership.

15. It takes more than education agencies to develop interprofessional collaborations.

16. Interprofessional collaboration is time consuming, difficult, complex, expensive, necessary, fun, and challenging.

17. Interprofessional education is not dependent on school-linked services; it is broader. Achieving intended outcomes requires more than school-linked services.

Recently, I asked my colleague, John (the Houston ISD principal), to share his thinking with me in regard to the difference between cooperation and collaboration. He began by pointing out that in the dictionary, these two words have the same definition. He continued by positing that in an educational setting, cooperation and collaboration must be distinct. Examples of cooperation are the common simple partnerships between schools and businesses, social services and government agencies, civic groups and parents. All too often, these partnerships involve only minimal responsibilities for the non-school partner from business, social services, or parents. It is a mistake to assume collaboration is taking place when these partners are busy with minimal tasks and responsibilities such as creating school calendars, serving as room mothers, directing students to the bus area, and hosting teacher lunches. As important as cooperation activities are, it is really collaborative kinds of partnerships that help drive effective teaching and learning in our schools.

Collaboration efforts strive to move beyond the day-to-day running of the school. Collaboration implies that we want to make a difference or a change and that we truly realize that we need the help of others to meet the challenges of educating our students. John ties his discussion about cooperation and collaboration to an interesting analogy:

It's kind of like the discussion we have about the difference between management and leadership. You know, we say that management involves such things as preparing the school budget, scheduling of classes and assignments, completing district and state reports, and keeping the buses running on time. But leadership, we say, involves tasks much more complex and [that] depend on our ability to solve problems, seek creative solutions, handle delicate personnel issues, monitor the delivery of appropriate and effective instruction, and other things considered to be the "messy challenges" of school leadership.

The following table illustrates how John looks at ordinary tasks and differentiates between cooperation and collaboration. To help with perspective, John thinks of cooperation as the "brainstorm" and collaboration as the "think tank." The "think tank" is where the "ah-ha's" occur.

**Table 6.1**    Cooperation vs. Collaboration

| Task | Cooperation— "Brainstorm" | Collaboration— "Think Tank" |
|---|---|---|
| Creating a subcommittee for the faculty advisory board of a school | To work out a problem about an employee dress code through creating a plan | To discover the leadership at your school by observing those employees who take a leadership role<br><br>Ah-ha:<br>"Ms. Rodriguez sure has a way of staying on task and she would be great on the shared decision making committee." |
| Creating a university bond of hourly volunteers with student teachers. | To assist children with aspiring teachers | To volunteer and become a teacher at your school with experience<br><br>Ah-ha:<br>"Sylvia has had time to discover the school climate, rituals, and celebrations and would be an asset to the school." |
| Creating opportunities for businesses to visit classrooms | To expose students to guest speakers from the business community | To become a resource for school supplies and other donations<br><br>Ah-ha:<br>"Joe's father works at a sign company and we sure would like a new school banner." |
| Creating a parent-teacher organization for fundraising | To provide an opportunity for parents to become part of school governance | To provide an opportunity for children to have their parents at school and raise their self-esteem<br><br>Ah-ha:<br>"Jennifer's mom raises money for our school and her husband manages a 15-story office building—our chocolate sales will soar." |

| Task | Cooperation— "Brainstorm" | Collaboration— "Think Tank" |
|---|---|---|
| Creating a vertical team with university curriculum departments | To meet the district needs and create a theoretical bond | To understand fully that what is done in one grade relies on what is done in another grade, through the eyes of a curriculum specialist |
| | | Ah-ha: "The curriculum department of Cummings University will be assisting our leadership roles by sharing their knowledge about algebra manipulatives." |
| Creating safety plans with local police and fire departments | To meet the district needs for current safety regulations | To create a loyalty with the police department and fire department to establish stronger safety procedures that later may involve parents |
| | | Ah-ha: "We need a volunteer crossing guard at the corner of Rampart and Glenmont." |
| Creating an understanding of assessment by parents | To present to parents the district goals and expectations | To be visible to parents and to find out more information about the parents that attend—knowing and planning with them paves a strong relationship for the child and teacher |
| | | Ah-ha: "Bob's father is an artist and we need a mural in the cafeteria." |

## CLOSING THOUGHTS

With the help of Dean Corregan and John Barrera, I hope I have provided an adequate description of the importance of collaboration for leading from below the surface. Collaboration is more important today than it was a few decades ago. Children now bring to school much more than purely educational needs. The percentage of children living in poverty continues to climb at an alarming rate. More suffer from neglect or abuse at home than ever before. The school leader is charged with being an instructional leader while at the same time dealing with more and more confounding variables coming from the periphery.

As educational, social, and health care concerns continue to grow and become more intermingled, school leaders must look below the surface to create a new kind of organizational structure: one built upon genuine collaborative partnerships among the school, university, businesses, civic groups, parents, social service agencies, and governmental agencies. The point is that we cannot do it alone. The message is clear: "No single profession or institution can assume the full responsibility for creating the conditions that children need to flourish" (Melaville & Blank, 1998, as cited in Corregan, 2001, p. 179).

## CHAPTER SEVEN

# *Looking Beyond the Obvious*

### FROM SUPERINTENDENT TO SECRETARY OF EDUCATION

Rod Paige, former Superintendent of the Houston Independent School District, was seen as "the great figure" and leader of the fourth-largest school district in the nation. Under Paige's leadership, the press was dramatic and inspiring: At every juncture, Paige was given recognition for outstanding leadership. When Paige left the district to become the U.S. Secretary of Education with the Bush administration, we all wondered what would happen to the Houston School District without its leader. Something very interesting *surfaced*.

The district not only successfully sustained momentum, but even seemed to make continued progress with improved student learning outcomes, national recognition from the Eli Broad Foundation for exemplary urban schools, and seminal work in the area of charter schools and vouchers.

Recall for a moment the Albert Schweitzer perspective mentioned earlier—"the sum of the small and obscure deeds is a thousand times stronger than the acts of those who receive wide, public recognition." Wow! Here is the great Albert Schweitzer telling us to look away from the great leaders—he compares their accomplishments to *foam* on the waves of a deep ocean, and instead focuses on the small and obscure deeds of others.

The real leader(s) of the Houston Independent School District were, and continue to be, the six area superintendents, the program coordinators, and the principals of the district's 342 schools. These people are far from the public foreground of the district, but it is they who have been solving problems and making a difference in the lives of students and teachers. These "below-the-surface leaders" accomplish their great works without public recognition.

## THE SAT STORY

We move now to an example certainly related to educational leadership, but focusing on a couple of university scholars who fully understand and practice "leading from below the surface." David Berliner and Bruce Biddle wrote *The Manufactured Crisis* in 1996, highlighting the myths, fraud, and attack on American public education. Their contention is that too often, concerns about education and plans for its improvement are not based on honest and informed evaluation of available evidence. The following SAT Story is told to show their ability to investigate beyond the *foam* and *below the surface* of glaring data.

To begin their story, Berliner and Biddle introduce their believed myth by quoting *A Nation at Risk* from 1983:

> For the first time in the history of our country, the educational skills of one generation will not surpass, will not equal, will not even approach those of their parents.
>
> Paul Copperman (1978)

Average achievement of high school students on most standardized tests is now lower than 26 years ago when Sputnik was launched.

> *A Nation at Risk* (National Commission
> on Excellence in Education, 1983, p. 8)

From 1950 to 1989, we probably experienced the worst educational decline in our history. Between 1963 and 1980, for example, combined average Scholastic Aptitude Test (SAT) scores in math and verbal fell 90 points, from 980 to 890.

> William Bennett
> (*The Devaluing of America*, 1992, p. 55)

Shortly after the publication of *A Nation at Risk,* several other reports came from government and industry repeating Bennett's claim of student achievement declining, as confirmed by standardized test records.

## Let's Look at the Data

Sure enough! Examining the data reveals a decline in SAT scores in both math and verbal components of the test from 1970 to 1997, shown in Figure 7.1.

### Looking Below the Foam

Here is where Berliner and Biddle further examine the data to reveal much more below the surface to explain the decline, pointing to how flawed the critics' claim of danger is. Listed below are their findings and interpretation:

1. First of all, the SAT measures math and verbal, but does not require student knowledge of history, the sciences, the arts, the social sciences, foreign language, the humanities, and other important subjects that high schools teach.

**Figure 7.1**    SAT Math and Verbal

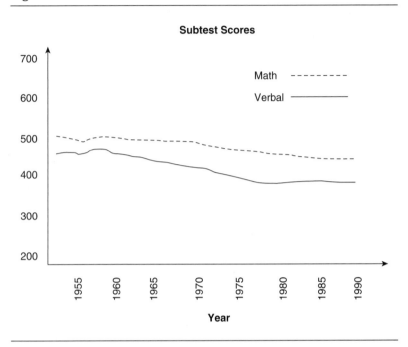

2. SAT scores are not reported as numbers of right answers, but are scaled in such a way that if an average student misses an answer in the middle range, that item might lower his score by 8–10 points; however, if an above-average student misses an answer in the upper range of score, he might have 50 points deducted from his total score. So to say SAT scores declined by 60–90 points, what does this really mean? (Even today, our local Houston newspapers report an annual change of one or two points as meaningful.)

3. SAT scores are meant to predict GPA in college, not to evaluate the achievements of teachers, schools, school districts, or school administrators.

4. Because the SAT is voluntary, some states have as many as 70% of high school seniors taking the SAT, while others report as low as 10% of seniors completing the test. This means that, in the states with 10% of seniors taking the test,

those seniors are likely to be students in the upper quartiles of ability and achievement; and states in which 70% of seniors take the test will have a greater number of students with weaker high school records. This is not a problem, but certainly it could explain a lowering of the national average.

5. The trend over the last few decades reveals more and more students taking the SAT (e.g., students in the lower quartiles of achievement, more students from minority groups). If more and more groups are in the pool, is it not likely that the averages might change?

6. What is really interesting is the fact that over the years, the scores for White and Asian students have remained steady, but scores for Blacks and Native Americans have actually climbed dramatically. Here is a below-the-surface reality—with the scores from the greatest number of students (White and Asian) remaining rather stable, and the smaller number of students (Black and Native American) making significant gains. Averaging all students' scores would not result in huge gains in averages.

Berliner and Biddle close this analysis by stating,

So although critics have trumpeted the alarming news that SAT scores fell during the late 1960s and early 1970s, this decline indicates nothing about the performance of American schools. Rather, it signals that students from a broader range of backgrounds were then getting interested in college, which should have been cause for celebration, not alarm. (p. 23)

## NOT SETTLING FOR EMBROIDERING THE EDGES

Though this next example may not highlight any individual leaders, I suggest it is helpful at this point to take a look at how some very large urban school districts deal with leading from below the surface. I am referencing the very recent work of William Ouchi, a professor in corporate renewal at the Anderson School of Management of the University of California, Los Angeles. Writing with coauthor Lydia Segal, Ouchi published *Making Schools Work* (2003).

Ouchi and Segal studied the three largest school districts in the country: New York City, Los Angeles, and Chicago. These three districts were compared to three radically decentralized school districts in Edmonton (Canada), Seattle, and Houston. In addition, they included the three largest archdiocesan systems, which are extremely decentralized: Chicago, New York, and Los Angeles. They were specifically interested in the popular claim by most districts that they have implemented decentralization of decision making.

One of their important findings suggests that the Los Angeles Unified School District may be "the worst school district in America" (p. 56). As evidence, they point to the fact that among California's 1,056 school districts, fourth and eighth graders in the L.A. Unified District are close to or in last place on the NAEP mathematics and reading tests, and in a similar position on the state standardized tests. In looking and analyzing *below the surface*, the researchers argue that the reasons for such a dismal performance have nothing to do with the students, the teachers, the budget, or the size of the district. Their conclusion? The problem is that the Los Angeles district has a system that centralizes all of the important decisions at headquarters.

Let me explain further why I think these two researchers have uncovered some effective large urban districts where leadership is practiced from below the surface. When looking at the data on the surface, we find practically every district in the nation reporting that they have implemented decentralization of decision making. And on the surface, all districts point to site-based management, parent advisory councils, teacher curriculum councils, and other practices as examples of decentralization of decision making. Below the surface, however, Ouchi points to the fact that this so-called decentralization "isn't the real thing, it's a phony" (p. 56). This phony decentralization encourages teachers, principals, and parents to spend hours and hours in planning and discussions but gives them no authority or money with which to implement their creative ideas. The culprit, Ouchi suggests, is the practice of "centralization" under the falsely claimed practice of decentralization. In *Education Week* (2003, p. 44), Ouchi presents "The 7 Keys to Success" in producing dramatically better student results, as found in his multiyear study of 223 schools in six public and three Catholic archdiocesan school districts. Let me summarize a few of them here to illustrate the strategies of getting below the surface.

*Every principal is an entrepreneur.* An entrepreneur, as opposed to a bureaucrat, is able to bend the rules to focus on student achievement. Bureaucrats follow the rules that are handed down to them from above. Centralized districts most often punish entrepreneurs and award bureaucrats. To encourage entrepreneurs, says Ouchi, "districts must reduce the number of central office staffs, and instead let schools have the money." He draws attention to the following:

> For example, the Archdiocese of Los Angeles serves about 100,000 students and has a central office staff of only 24, including secretaries. By comparison, the Los Angeles Unified School District has 733,000 students and a central office staff of 11,896. In addition to having too many bureaucrats telling schools what to do, this means that Los Angeles spends 35.4 percent of its budget on teacher pay, while Houston spends 48.5 percent and Edmonton spends 55.8 percent on teachers. (p. 44)

*Every school controls its own budget.* Ouchi's research shows that in the three centralized districts, New York City principals control only 6.1% of the money spent in their schools, Los Angeles principals control 6.7% of their school budget, and Chicago principals control 19.3%. In contrast, in the three decentralized school districts, Houston principals control 58.6% of their budget, Seattle principals control 79.3%, and in

Edmonton, principals control an astonishing 91.7% of the money spent in their schools.

*Parents can choose among a variety of unique schools.* In the three decentralized school districts, Ouchi found that a prevailing characteristic was the choice parents had within the district to enroll their child in one of several schools. These districts realize that no two schools should be alike, and no two neighborhoods or school missions are alike. Summarizing his research, Ouchi states,

> Don't settle for embroidering the edges of your school district. What's needed is deep, basic, revolutionary. It's succeeded in Edmonton, Seattle, and Houston, and it can succeed in your school district. (p. 44)

## Concluding Thoughts

As stated earlier, I have come to view leadership not so much as something to be learned, but rather something that *is* learning. Leading from below the surface is hard work and takes time and practice to accomplish. Most importantly, it does not occur naturally but requires diligent and constant focus on the unique collection of students in each of our schools. What makes this kind of leadership even more difficult is the fact that most school environments and the "powers that be" do not encourage or reward such leadership. But I am somewhat certain of one thing: The leaders of the great schools mentioned in this chapter and throughout this book face their uphill battles with courage and conviction, and the decisions they make are made because they care about helping all students be successful.

**Below the Surface**

- Careful, cautious decision making; bending, not breaking rules; managing political capital
- Evidence-based decision making
- Strategy
- Collaboration: beyond cooperation
- Looking below the obvious
- **Practicing leadership**

CHAPTER EIGHT

# Creating Leadership Behaviors

## A Leadership Practice Field

In William Isaacs's *Dialogue and the Art of Thinking Together* (1999, p. 31), he uses a model (shown in Figure 8.1) to illustrate the three fundamental levels of human interaction. Though he is writing about the art of effective dialogue, I suggest his model is especially powerful in discussing leadership from below the surface. Let me also suggest that his three components or levels of human interaction are also key in creating leadership practice fields. More on leadership practice fields later in this chapter, but allow me first to describe Isaacs's three levels of human interaction and how they relate to the subject of this book.

1. *Capacity for new behavior.* The field of educational leadership and more specifically principal preparation programs (in the universities) have long suffered from irrelevance to the day-to-day job of the school principal. Recently, more than ever, our critics point to the disconnect that exists between university

**Figure 8.1**

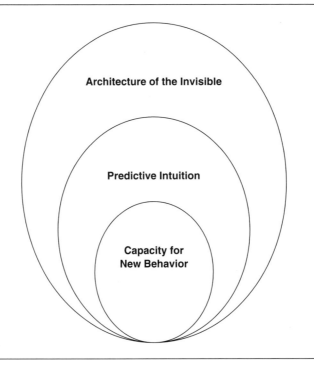

principal preparation and what principals really have to do on the job. As in Isaacs's dialogic approach, leading from below the surface requires that "we must learn to be aware of the contradictions between what we say and what we do" (p. 30). Developing "capacity for new behavior" helps us address ambiguity and begin to practice leadership skills more centered on teaching and student learning. I will return to specific ways we can develop this capacity for new behavior later. Stay with me as I present Isaacs's other two levels.

2. *Predictive intuition.* School leaders do not always see the forces operating below the surface. This can cause us to misunderstand

FIGURE SOURCE: From *Dialogue and the Art of Thinking Together*, by William Isaacs, Copyright 1999 by William Isaacs. Used by permission of Doubleday, a division of Random House, Inc.

and misinterpret both what others are doing and the influence we ourselves are likely to have on situations related to teaching and learning. This leads to the realization that our efforts to improve and change instruction and learning are neutralized or stymied by others who do not share our vision of effective teaching and learning. Isaacs suggests, and I agree with him, "that it is possible to develop an intuitive understanding of the nature of these forces, and to develop ways of anticipating and managing them" (p. 30). Predictive intuition allows us to see more clearly the forces below the surface and helps to align thinking and working together.

3. *Architecture of the invisible.* As leaders, teachers, and students work together, we must be aware that each person's thinking takes place in our own space or atmosphere. This space consists of our thinking and understanding. We have a tendency to work only in our own space and neglect the invisible space of others. Isaacs invites us to "become more conscious of the invisible atmosphere of others" (p. 30).

To help understand how the interaction of these three levels can make us better leaders from below the surface, let me share an experience I had as a principal of a small, rural K–8 school district in central California. This district had traditionally ended classroom instruction every Friday following lunch. The afternoon time was used for sports practice: Coaches and students used the three hours to practice basketball, football, volleyball, or baseball, according to the season and time of year. When our school's team competed with other schools in the area, these games also took place on Friday afternoon. Regular classroom teachers often took their remaining students (non-sports participators) to the fields to watch either the practices or games with other schools. The point here is that no real instruction took place at this school from 11:00 A.M. until 3:30 P.M. each and every Friday of the school year.

The superintendent and I agreed that this situation needed to change. Based on the 180-day school year, students and teachers were missing more than 540 classroom instruction hours. After further discussion with the school board, we decided to restructure our Friday afternoons. Much discussion took place with the teachers, who agreed on the change. The change essentially moved the practices to after school each afternoon (coaches were paid additional stipends). We did agree to keep the actual games on Friday afternoons, and allow students and teachers to attend. The trade-off seemed to be the best for all: Much of the time on Fridays went back to classroom instruction, and the community and students could continue to support our teams on Friday afternoon for the actual competitions with other schools.

Made sense both educationally and ethically, right? Well, needless to say, in the days, weeks, and months to follow, a ground-swelling of opposition surfaced, which included letters to the principal, superintendent, and board, threatening ACLU involvement, teacher union intervention, and even protesting at the Friday afternoon games. The demands were for a return to the weekly free Friday afternoons. Since most of the letters were unsigned, we began to investigate the source of such protests. On the surface, we found that the coaches were not real happy with the arrangement, since it meant hours after school for them (and the stipends were unsatisfactory). Also on the surface, we discovered that many in the community enjoyed coming out on Friday afternoons to watch the practices and support the players. The board approved a higher stipend for coaches, and the superintendent and I spent much time out in the community explaining the importance of instructional time, both from our perspective and the law from the State Department regulating hours of instruction. Soon, both coaches and community members felt better about and accepted the change. End of the ground-swelling opposition? Not in the least!

Eventually, we discovered that "below the surface" was the student government president, along with a teacher representative for the teachers union, secretively talking with other teachers and community members, arguing that the administration was not being fair to student interests and not supporting sports in the curriculum. Wow, we had no idea!

You can imagine the time and effort spent to finally resolve the Friday afternoon dilemma, but in retrospect, I think of Isaacs's three levels of human interaction. Recall from our previous discussion predictive intuition: We do not always see the forces operating below the surface, causing misunderstanding and misinterpretation both about what others are doing and what influence we ourselves are having. And in terms of architecture of the invisible, we neglect the "invisible space of others," failing to talk with *all* the significant others. We were focused on our "certainties" in our space, while ignoring the space of others.

## OK, ON TO A LEADERSHIP PRACTICE FIELD

To help us understand the nature and importance of a leadership practice field, let me devote some time to illustrating an analogy on the golf course. What follows is my colleague (Don Coleman) discussing his mastery of the game of golf (Coleman & Creighton, 2002, pp. 16–21).

> Three months ago, I once again began playing golf after a 30-year hiatus. I cannot begin to explain how badly I played. I embarrassed myself every time I visited the course. I did not want to play with anyone I knew because my scores were so high. I intentionally wore a floppy hat that I could pull down low so no one would recognize me. Yes, it was that bad. I could walk past people I knew but they never recognized me.
>
> I spent a lot of time practicing shots on the driving range. However, hitting balls on the driving range is not an acceptable substitute for playing on the course. Indeed, driving range play provides a false sense of optimism, an optimism that fades quickly when returning to the course.
>
> During my trips to and from the driving range and courses, I would reflect on [the relationship of] my experiences with golf to my life as professor of education administration. When one looks across golf courses, as in schools, one cannot tell the "golfers" from the "hackers"

until watching them play or checking their scores. All of the players may be nattily dressed and carrying a nice set of clubs in a good looking bag, but none of these detractors compensate for the scores achieved. Likewise, we cannot tell the hackers from the professionals among school leaders, until we learn the score.

One day, while at the course, I was assigned to play with a 92-year-old man who used only a six-iron around the entire course, including putting, and he beat me. That day, out of desperation, I asked the kids in the club house if they had a professional on staff. They recommended one who they thought would be a good teacher for me; a young fellow who had just come off the professional circuit and who was supposedly an excellent teacher. I made an appointment to see the "professor" the next day on the driving range. He gave me a bucket of balls and told me to go out and start hitting a few irons to warm up. The first thing he said was, "You really have a nice swing. I suspect you are not a beginner." We visited a bit about my earlier experiences and recent trials before he asked to see how I was gripping the club.

The next thing he did was give me a lecture on the technology that went into the making of the clubs that I had purchased. I listened closely as he gave me all the "theoretical junk" instead of something practical that I could use. He explained in theoretical detail what I was doing that was causing my difficulties with the clubs. He also indicated that my scores were probably worsening because the harder I would try, the more I exacerbated the problem. He also warned, "You are going to feel uncomfortable for a while, learning the new grip and stance, but give it time and practice."

Eager to try what I had learned, I went back to the golf course. Within a month, I knocked off 10–12 strokes per 18 holes. While my iron play improved, I was still dissatisfied with my woods. So, I went back to the "professor" for another lesson. Again, he gave me a theoretical lesson on the clubs I was using as well as my grip, distance from the club head and stance. He said, "You have the basics now. You must do a lot of practice to feel comfortable with the clubs, the grip, and the stance. You should see additional improvement fairly soon."

In another month, I had knocked an additional 10 strokes off my round scores. His explanations taught me what I must do each time I "address" the ball to improve my performance, but the practice requires additional time developing new skills with the required knowledge. He provided me with substantive knowledge and skill instruction, but the application and skill development are still up to me.

To increase time for practicing, I have now stopped playing golf 18 holes at a time. I have also stopped going to the driving range. Instead I have implemented a strategy that seems to work better. I play the back nine holes at a local course early in the morning while the golfers and other "hackers" begin their trek around the front nine. I spend my time hitting two or three extra balls from various lies I achieve. By hitting essentially the same shot two or three additional times, I see that better shots are within my realm of possibility, but only with considerable extra practice.

When I play a regular 18-hole round now with the "hackers," I receive accolades about how my game has improved. I can also see that additional lessons will be needed to reduce my scores further in the future, but I must also devote additional time in diligent practice. (p. 18)

## Defining a Practice

Coleman's analogy of his experiences on the golf course to school administration is excellent and points to the importance of practice in our profession.

A practice is an activity that you do repeatedly to achieve a particular experience or outcome. For example, students of sports (e.g., tennis or basketball), music (e.g., violin or piano), and medicine (e.g., interns) spend hours and hours practicing. This practice has a deliberate design and intention that, when used well, produces a defined result: competitive skill, musical accuracy and interpretation, and the ability to perform medical diagnosis and treatment.

I can think of no other profession that fails to value or provide sufficient opportunities for new professionals to practice—in a different kind of space where one can practice and learn. The medical profession has a practice field, musicians and dancers have a practice field, the New York Nicks have a practice field, pilots and astronauts have a practice field, and on and on—but do we really have a practice field in school administration? I argue that we do not—and the internship as we know it is a sorry excuse for one. Murphy (1999) reported that although supervised practice could be the most critical phase of the administrator's preparation, the component is notoriously weak. Murphy claims that field-based practices do not involve an adequate number of experiences and are arranged on the basis of convenience.

For some time, I have argued for the implementation of a "leadership practice field" into our preparation programs. The conceptual notion at work here is that of creating a bridge between a performance field (working *in* the system) and a practice field (working *on* the system). This model is based on the work of Daniel Kim, a colleague of Peter Senge (*The Fifth Discipline*) and cofounder of the MIT Organizational Learning Center, where he is currently director of the Learning Laboratory Research Project. The central idea is that a leadership practice field provides an environment where a prospective leader can experiment with alternative strategies and policies, test assumptions, and practice working through the complex issues of school leadership in a constructive and productive manner (Kim, 1995).

Kim is fond of using the following scenario as an introduction to the "practice field" concept:

Imagine you are walking across a tightrope stretched between two skyscraper buildings in Chicago. The wind is blowing and the rope is shaking as you inch your way forward. One of your teammates sits in the wheelbarrow you are balancing in front of you, while another colleague sits on your shoulders. There are no safety nets, no harnesses. You think to yourself, "One false move and the three of us will take an express elevator straight down to the street." Suddenly your trainer yells from the other side, "Try a new move! Experiment! Take some risks! Remember, you are a learning team!" (Kim, 1995, p. 353)

Kim continues by admitting the ludicrous nature of this scenario, but emphasizes that this is precisely what many companies expect their management teams to do—experiment and learn in an environment that is risky, turbulent, and unpredictable. And unlike musicians, medical students, or sports teams, management teams do not have an adequate practice field; they are nearly always on the performance field.

I suggest this scenario truly resembles the life of school principals, and the concept of a practice field is applicable to the field of educational administration and especially its preparation programs. Except for a brief experience with some form of internship, notoriously considered weak and suffering from a lack of quality and relevance, where do prospective school leaders get an opportunity to leave the day-to-day pressures of school administration and enter a different kind of space where they can practice and learn?

You as practicing principals continue to tell us that what you do in your jobs in schools bears little resemblance to your preparation received at the university. You also share your frustration with having so little time to be proactive: You are constantly required to be *re*active. Principals have little time and even less opportunity to practice their skills in "safe-failing" places. Even finding time for reflection is difficult in the nonstop, hectic pace of a principal's day.

## A PRACTICE FIELD FURTHER DEFINED

Several authors have suggested we need to view leadership more as a performing art rather than as a specific set of skills, competencies, and knowledge (Sarason, 1999; Vaill, 1989).

When practicing a symphony, the conductor can have the orchestra *slow down* the tempo in order to practice certain sections. A medical student in residence has the opportunity to slow down and practice certain medical procedures and diagnoses. The Los Angeles Lakers spend most of their time in a practice field, slowing down the tempo and practicing certain moves, strategies, and assumptions.

All of these practice fields exist in an environment with opportunities for making mistakes, in a "safe-failing space to enhance learning" (Kim, 1995). When and where do aspiring or practicing school principals get a chance to slow down and practice certain moves or aspects of their jobs?

Argyris and Schön (1978), in their book, *Organizational Learning*, posit that leaders function with a gap between their conceptual belief of the right course of action and what they actually choose to do in the real situation. Not choosing to narrow or close these gaps can have two effects. It can (a) prohibit actual learning and (b) sustain the existing irrelevancy between principal preparation programs and effective leadership in the field. A leadership practice field can help identify and close such gaps. Here lies one of the most important reasons for leadership practice fields: School leaders are provided opportunities to connect what they conceptually believe is the right course of action to what they choose to do under real circumstances.

## PRACTICING LEADING FROM BELOW THE SURFACE

So will university preparation programs implement leadership practice fields? Not likely! And certainly not soon. The wheels of change in university preparation programs move slowly.

To fully illustrate, I must return to Isaacs's work on "building capacity for new behavior" (1999, p. 79). Now, remember he is talking about the art of dialogue, and I am making the connection to leading from below the surface. Isaacs suggests that the four practices serving as building blocks to building new behavior include (1) listening, (2) respecting,

(3) suspending, and (4) voicing. During my many years as a school administrator and now as a professor in education leadership preparation, I have noticed that effective school leaders possess these same four characteristics. They know how to listen, they continually respect, they are experts at suspending their certainties, and they fully realize that what they say or do not say has a powerful impact on the control and stability of the school organization. For the purposes of this chapter, I will only highlight the first two of Isaacs's building blocks for new behavior: listening and respecting.

## PRACTICING LISTENING

The eye seems to perceive at a superficial level. While the eye sees at the surface, the ear tends to penetrate below the surface. (Isaacs, p. 86)

Attend local school district board meetings or faculty meetings, but it is important you attend at a time when you have no part in the agenda. Sit in the back someplace, and just listen. Who is talking? What are they saying? How much do you hear about important issues like effective teaching and learning? Are people really listening to each other, or just talking to their point of view?

Practicing listening is not easy: First of all, you must work hard to create opportunities to practice the skill. So much of our school day is focused on *seeing* things, and we must purposely "slow down" to listen. We must also guard against the trap of interjecting our own "certainties" or "position" as we listen to others.

In my experience over the years, I cannot recall an image or memory of an effective school leader who did not have this very noticeable ability to listen before making decisions.

Isaacs argues (and I agree) that observing with our eyes results in only one layer of what really is occurring. Only through listening do we get further into the multiple layers of reality. On more occasions than I want to admit as a school leader, I made judgments about a teacher or high school student based entirely on what I observed with my eyes.

## PRACTICING RESPECTING

What exactly does it mean to respect someone? We must first realize that respecting is not a passive act; it is a purposeful and intentional act. Isaacs points out that the word comes from the Latin *respecere,* which means "to look again." When we first observe someone, we form certain judgments, but when looking again, we often see things we missed the first time. It is this second look that helps us get "below the surface" of first impressions.

At the university, I am involved in a program that takes a cohort of doctoral students each year on an international internship to schools in Mexico. Students (and I myself) possess several certainties about the poverty and low quality of instruction in Mexican schools. Without exception, during our experience there, and especially upon our return, we develop a tremendous *respect* for both the teachers and students in Mexico. It took a second look, or below-the-surface look, to really gain a new respect for both the people and the education.

Again, just as with listening, practicing respect is not an easy task and does not happen without intent. Here is something you can try to help focus on respecting. At a recent faculty meeting, my colleague Barbara Polnick introduced us to the book, *A Peacock in the Land of Penguins,* by Gallagher Hateley and Warren Schmidt (2001). The theme of the book centers around the usual practice of organizations expecting (sometimes forcing) all employees to look alike.

> The story is about Perry the Peacock—a bright, talented, colorful bird—who comes to live in the Land of Penguins. He soon runs into problems because the penguins have established a chilly organizational climate that is formal, bureaucratic, and governed by a vast array of written and unwritten rules. His different and unusual style makes

the penguins feel uneasy. The very thing he was recruited for—his distinctive flair and creativity—is now viewed as a problem for the penguins, once he is in the organization.

Barbara helped us understand the importance of organizations allowing and even encouraging peacocks and other exotic birds to coexist for the good of the organization. As we analyzed our individual interests and characteristics, we as a faculty mainly identified with two specific birds: doves and hawks. Table 8.1 displays some characteristics of our two groups.

Now, here is where the practice of *respecting* began. Barbara asked the doves and the hawks to assemble in their respective groups and address the following question: What would you like the other group to know about you? In other words, in an indirect way, Barbara was asking us to consider *respecting* others who may not quite look like us.

**Table 8.1**    A Peacock in the Land of Penguins

DOVES

1. A dove is not one to be assertive over others.
2. A dove tends to speak indirectly and often seeks the opinion of others.
3. Doves are thoughtful, sensitive, and caring.
4. A dove hates conflict, tension, and confrontation.
5. Doves want to be appreciated for their participation and service.

HAWKS

1. Hawks tend to speak quickly and directly.
2. Hawks get impatient if things aren't progressing as quickly as they'd like.
3. A hawk likes to set lots of goals, work alone, and work on several projects at once.
4. A hawk dislikes wasting time, and enjoys competition, pressure, and challenging work.
5. Hawks like to be appreciated for their accomplishments.

Something interesting began to happen as the doves reported:

1. We sometimes feel like we're being ignored. We really just need to be accepted for who we are and want to feel like we're needed.

2. We feel embarrassed when we're challenged by assertive others.

3. You need to let us work in collaborative groups, working on team projects and group activities. When you ask us to do things separately, we feel helpless.

Listening as one of the hawks, I was awed by the honesty expressed by the doves. I never thought much before about how different they are—but different in a good way. I began to think about how my behavior, as a hawk, was perhaps stifling their creativity and effectiveness.

We (the hawks) presented our short list of things we wanted the doves to know about us:

1. Please understand that we mean no disrespect, we just work fast and have to move quickly to get to all the projects we are responsible for.

2. We don't feel good with "small talk," but prefer to discuss what we want to achieve and the results we're going to accomplish.

3. To be productive, we need to work alone sometimes, and don't really mean to distance ourselves.

During our presentation, I was equally awed by the looks of *respect* coming from the other side of the room (the doves). It occurred to me then that each group was beginning to respect each other. I also realized that this was not going to be easy and would have to be practiced, and practiced, and practiced. Now, two months later, I see continued signs of mutual respect across the diverse styles of our 11 faculty members.

Through more practice, I suspect we will see that sometimes conflict and confrontation is OK and can be positive and constructive. And we will grow professionally by developing tolerance for diversity, honest disagreements, and healthy debate.

So what does all this mean and imply to you, the practicing or aspiring school leader? In the next chapter, I will attempt to tie all the previous chapters together and present significant rationale and reasons for us to lead from below the surface.

# Implications for Practicing School Administrators

The primary purpose of education is to provide knowledge to help individuals, groups, and entire societies improve their lives and the lives of others (The Education Resources Institute, 1996).

This goal sounds obvious and simple enough. But is it?

Never in the history of our educational enterprise has the school leader been faced with such complex responsibilities and so many change forces, both internal and external. Before we get into some of these forces, let's agree up front that we do not view these forces as insurmountable roadblocks to effectively leading schools. On the contrary, we want to direct each one of these negative forces into a positive force. Though the list of forces we deal with may be limitless, and somewhat situational, I have chosen to highlight two specific external forces that I feel are timely and critical, setting up a demand for a different kind of leadership (from below the surface).

For the purposes of this final chapter, I have chosen not to address the internal forces in our administrative lives, such as school boards, community activists, other administrators, staff and faculty, students, or existing programs and structures. Instead, I want to highlight external forces for the following reasons:

1. Leading from below the surface requires more attention to external forces than we traditionally give them.

2. Internal forces, though troublesome, seem to be more visible and obvious, and quite frankly, I think we are getting pretty good at dealing with them.

In the rapidly changing world we live in, two specific external forces have hit us almost overnight. I'd like to shape my discussion of the implications for practicing school administrators around these two external forces: (1) the demands for greater accountability, and (2) the increased use of the Internet and the way online learning is changing our schools.

## ACCOUNTABILITY

The demand for greater accountability for student achievement from our politicians and legislators is heard daily, now influencing every decision we make as school leaders. There is not one among us who is against accountability that enhances teaching and learning. But we all, leading from below the surface, must concern ourselves with what an accountability system should look like and consist of. Much of the research literature indicates the accountability measures have been imposed on students, teachers, schools, and school districts, and were developed and implemented without our consent or involvement (Waite, Boone, & McGhee, 2001). No discussion can occur today without considering the recent No Child Left Behind (NCLB) Act of 2001, reauthorizing the Elementary and Secondary Education Act (ESEA) of 1965.

NCLB can be lauded for its emphasis on standards-based reform and the encouragement for states to adapt ambitious and rigorous subject-matter standards. In addition, attention is paid to the importance of all children, and promoting the learning of groups of students that have lagged behind in the past.

Those of us who lead from below the surface must address a more hidden feature of NCLB: the question of what accountability means. The underlying assumption of NCLB is that tests and testing measure accountability. Though requirements include some reliable measures such as graduation and dropout rates, the student measures that count in NCLB are dominated by tests of reading and language arts and mathematics.

None of us is questioning the importance of reading and mathematics. But we need to seriously question the logic of using tests as an exclusive measure of student achievement— particularly when it is limited to only two subject areas (it is somewhat encouraging to learn that science will be added later, in selected grades). We discussed in an earlier chapter that much evidence exists to indicate that teachers place greater emphasis on material that is covered on a test than they do on other material or subjects, sacrificing precious time from other, equally important curricular areas.

## LEADING FROM BELOW THE SURFACE

Here, lying below the surface, are a few other areas of concern, needing our careful attention and further investigation:

1. Is it possible that this increased pressure from *accountability* and *testing* (two terms that have unfortunately and incorrectly become synonymous) may be forcing more of our quality teachers from the profession? Incidentally, my own daughter, a third-grade teacher in Houston, Texas, has on more than one occasion confessed her frustration with this obvious and intentional pressure from testing, and has questioned her own career as a teacher. We already know that many teachers who leave are among the brightest and most creative, "exactly those most likely to chafe under the yoke of tighter state control of curriculum and instruction" (Kohn, 2000, as cited in Waite et al., 2001, p. 192).

2. Is it possible that this increased pressure from *accountability* and *testing* may be influencing the decision of such large

numbers of certified principals to not enter school administration positions, and influencing *currently practicing* principals to exit their positions prematurely? In Steinberg's (2000) article on the scarcity of building principals across the nation, the author notes, "During the movement to improve schools that has swept through classrooms in the past decade, the principal has become as visibly accountable as a football coach, and must suffer the wrath of parents and state monitors" (p. 72). I find it equally disconcerting to report that already many districts (e.g., Houston ISD) across the nation are providing monetary incentive bonuses to principals who raise and/or sustain student test scores. I argue that there may be an ethical issue here: for example, are we saying that perhaps a principal should be able to purchase a new car or stereo on the shoulders of students who perform well on tests?

3. Is it possible that the method of measuring accountability (i.e., standardized test scores) is too shallow? Past research evidence and experience suggest that the measures that enter into the accountability system "should be broadly and deeply conceived and provide information on a wide range of outcome, contextual, and process variables" (Linn, 2003, p. 3).

To effectively lead from below the surface, it is not enough to just recognize and agree that accountability measures should be considered; we must insist that the powers that be (our legislators and politicians) consider the evidence (research) and our input before they implement any legislation geared toward school improvement.

I want to now turn to a second area that I feel has powerful implications for practicing school administrators who want to lead from below the surface: technology implementation for the improvement of teaching and learning.

## THE DISJUNCTURE BETWEEN SOCIETAL USE AND SCHOOL USE OF TECHNOLOGY

In an earlier writing (Creighton, 2003, p. xi), I suggest that school districts and school leaders must realize that what we are currently doing with technology can be likened to "putting lipstick on a bulldog" (Kanter, 2001). On the surface we assume we are using the Internet and Web design in highly productive ways. This kind of makeup job (boxes and wires) does not work. The bulldog doesn't suddenly become beautiful simply because it is forced to wear lipstick. Nothing else about the bulldog or its behavior has changed. Many schools are guilty of putting up a Web site or two, and investing in fancy hardware and software, thinking they are technologically advanced. Don't misunderstand me—I strongly believe that the use of technology in our schools has the potential for significant and radical educational reform, but only if we get below the surface of fancy computer labs and slick Web pages. Much evidence exists indicating technology has not significantly changed the ways teachers teach; instead, most technology mirrors traditional instructional pedagogy. And much worse, examples abound showing that technology in the classroom can be used as a disguise for poor teaching.

When looking at how we use technology in our day-to-day living, we see at every corner examples of how technology has changed the way we work, shop, travel, communicate, cook, raise crops, manufacture goods, and engage in recreation (Guthrie, 2003).

> Ironically, although instructional technology has had an equal capacity for dramatic change, its day-to-day deployment in public school classrooms has lagged its potential dramatically. (p. 54)

Here are two frequently heard arguments:

1. Some say we have lagged behind because of a supply issue: We need more computers and Internet connections in our schools. We must reduce the computer-to-child ratio so we can effectively implement technology. Interesting, but let's look at some recent data (evidence). Cuban (2001) reports that in 1981, there was one computer per 125 students. By 1991, this ratio had changed to 18 students per computer, and in 2003, there was one computer for every 4 students.

OK, what about access to the Internet? The evidence reveals an equally conflicting case. In 1994, only 3% of American classrooms had access to the Internet. In 1999, the access increased to 64%, and in 2003, approximately 94% of school classrooms had Internet access (Palloff & Pratt, 2003).

2. A second argument often heard from our teachers (and fellow administrators), and one presented by Larry Cuban (2001), is that our lagging use of technology is related to teachers' instructional responsibilities. This author argues that we have done it again: We have shown teachers and students that we are pretty good at addition, but have not subtracted anything.

> The teacher's workdays, allocation of time, career rewards and incentives, interactions with each other, parents, and students are simply not altered in any meaningful way by technology. Hence, computers and other technologies remain on the periphery of classrooms, and isolated in computer labs in schools, because teachers see no need to alter what they do to accomplish what is routinely expected of them. (Guthrie, 2003, p. 59)

As leaders from below the surface, we must ask this one basic yet complex question: Why is there this obvious disconnect between how our modern society has implemented technology and how our schools have yet to take full advantage of technology to improve teaching and student learning?

## THE VIRTUAL CLASSROOM

Let me continue by highlighting one additional concern I have myself and suggest that this has powerful and critical implications for us as practicing school leaders.

As a building principal in the early 1990s, I was involved in the use of online learning to help our small rural school district offer a few high school students some special courses in advanced math and pre-college composition. Through the use of Internet and video conferencing, we could offer advanced placement courses to students whose schools did not have enough students or a teacher for that particular class.

Online courses and even degrees earned online are fairly common for our college-age students. The "typical" online student is generally described as being older than 25 years of age, employed, a parent or guardian, with some higher education already attained, and equally likely to be either male or female (Gilbert, 2001, p. 74). However, recent data published by the National Center for Education Statistics (2002) report that as of December 31, 1999, as many as 65% of those age 18 and younger had enrolled in an online course, indicating the increasing popularity of virtual high school courses.

But what we see below the surface is not only the common offering of online courses to secondary students, but more alarming perhaps, the offering of courses to elementary-grade students. The proponents of home schooling in California, Ohio, Pennsylvania, and other states have recently used charter school regulations to launch *cyber schools* (Maeroff, 2003). The home schooling option is growing at an alarming rate, with many elementary students taking their entire curriculum at home (Hail, 2003).

Looking below the surface, we must focus on two ramifications, among many others: (1) the impact of the virtual classroom on elementary-age children, and (2) the new breed of competing instructional providers. Let me close this chapter on my suggested implications for practicing school leaders with my thoughts on these two concerns.

The growing number of elementary-age students participating in online learning should be a major concern for us, as leaders from below the surface. None of us would disagree that education is about mastering subjects, but we would also agree there is more. What about character development, socialization skills and opportunities, and working collaboratively with others of the same age? And if, as evidence suggests, elementary schools help lay the foundation for such qualities and characteristics, should we not be concerned about our ever-increasing cyber schools? Earlier, I mentioned a disconnect between how society is using technology and how schools are lagging behind. True perhaps, and schools should reflect the same degree of technology implementation as found in society. However, as we press on with sorting out this disconnect, we must remember that education is essentially a social force (Papalewis, 2000) and has all the complications that occur in a social environment. Are there implications here for practicing school administrators? I certainly think so.

There are many new forms of educating our youth emerging on the landscape, from public and private charters, cyber schools, and for-profit ventures such as the Edison Schools among others. These newer types or "new breeds" have evolved to fill newly identified needs of students that our traditional public schools, for whatever reason, have not met.

In looking at the new breed of technology providers of education, whether cyber schools or online instruction coming from independent schools, contracting, or vouchers, it is not competition that we fear. Understanding and looking below the surface of these new-breed alternatives is important to us as practicing school leaders for two reasons. First, these alternative providers represent competition. For each child disappearing from our attendance roster, $3,000–$5,000 (depending on district/state revenue limit) is lost from our operating budget. As much as we want to downplay competition, the truth is that competition does exist and we have no choice but to confront it head-on. Second, we must view an understanding of our competition as an opportunity to improve our existing schools. Let me provide a brief example.

During the early 1990s, I worked at the University of Wyoming and met Superintendent of Natrona County Schools (Casper, Wyoming) Chip Zallinger. He was gravely concerned about the great number of home schoolers in his district. Doing his math, he calculated a lost revenue of approximately $500,000 (100 students × $5,000). Looking below the surface, he discovered evidence that most of the parents of these kids were unhappy with the fact that the district curriculum did not focus on the basics—specifically, the *core knowledge* presented in E. D. Hirsch's *The Schools We Need* (1996).

To make a long story short, Zallinger presented a plan to the School Board: adopt a "school of choice" program, and allow interested teachers, parents, and administrators to present proposals to the board for consideration. A proposal for a magnet-type school designed around the research of E. D. Hirsch, with a curriculum emphasizing hard work, the learning of facts, and rigorous testing, was accepted by the board. The school opened with a full enrollment, consisting of many of the students previously home-schooled. Zallinger's plan resulted in the return of approximately 100 students and accompanying revenue to the district's budget. Fort Casper Academy continues today as a very successful school of choice in Casper, Wyoming.

So we come to the grand paradox of leading from below the surface with regard to accountability and technology: The potential of each presents both the greatest opportunity and the greatest threat to schools and their leaders. If we continue on the same path, we run the risk of not only wasting a lot of time and money in the process, but missing the opportunity of positively affecting the minds and lives of children. On the other hand, if we insist on implementing substantive and reliable accountability and technology plans to improve achievement and opportunities for all students, we stand to increase the tip of the iceberg appearing above the surface.

# References

American Educational Research Association. (2001). AERA position statement concerning high-stakes testing in preK–12 education. Retrieved February 20, 2001, from www.aera.net/about/policy/stakes.htm

Argyris, C., & Schön, D. (1978). *Organizational learning: A theory of action perspective.* Reading, MA: Addison-Wesley.

Badaracco, J. (2002). *Leading quietly: An unorthodox guide to doing the right thing.* Boston: Harvard Business School Press.

Bennett, W. (1992). *The devaluing of America: The fight for our culture and our children.* New York: Summit Books.

Berliner, D., & Biddle, B. (1996). *The manufactured crisis: Myths, fraud, and the attack on America's public schools.* New York: Addison-Wesley.

Bolman, L., & Deal, T. (1984). *Modern approaches to understanding and managing organizations.* San Francisco: Jossey-Bass.

Bourdieu, P. (1990). *The logic of practice.* Cambridge, UK: Polity Press.

Boyer, E. (1991). *Ready to learn: A mandate for the nation.* Princeton, NJ: Carnegie Foundation for the Advancement of Teaching.

Burns, J. (1978). *Leadership.* New York: Harper & Row.

Coleman, D., & Creighton, T. (2002). Bringing university education preparation programs up to par. *Education Leadership Review, 3*(1), 16–20.

Commission on Presidential Debates. (2000). The first 2000 Gore-Bush presidential debate: October 3, 2000. Retrieved January 24, 2001, from www.debates.org/pages/trans2000a.html

Copperman, P. (1978). *The literacy hoax: The decline of reading, writing, and learning in the public schools and what we can do about it.* New York: Morrow.

Corregan, D. (2001). The changing role of schools and higher education institutions with respect to community-based interagency collaboration and interprofessional partnerships. *Peabody Journal of Education, 75*(3), 176–195.

Creighton, T. (2001). *Schools and data: The educator's guide to using data to improve decision making.* Thousand Oaks, CA: Corwin Press.

Creighton, T. (2003). *The principal as technology leader.* Thousand Oaks, CA: Corwin Press.

Cuban, L. (2001). *Oversold and underused: Computers in the classroom.* Cambridge, MA: Harvard University Press.

Cushner, K., McClelland, A., & Safford, P. (2003). *Human diversity in education: An integrative approach* (4th ed.). New York: McGraw-Hill.

Deal, T. (1987). Effective school principals: Counselors, engineers, pawnbrokers, poets . . . or instructional leaders? In W. Greenfield (Ed.), *Instructional leadership: Concepts, issues, and controversies* (p. 230–245). Boston: Allyn & Bacon.

Deal, T., & Kennedy, A. (1982). *Corporate cultures.* Reading, MA: Addison-Wesley.

The Education Resources Institute (1996). *What is opportunity? A concept paper.* Boston: The Institute for Higher Education Policy.

Fiedler, F., & Chemers, M. (1984). *Improving leadership effectiveness: The leader match concept* (2nd ed.). New York: Wiley.

Gilbert, S. (2001). *How to be a successful online student.* New York: McGraw-Hill.

Guthrie, J. (2003). The historic paradox of instructional technology and education policy: A commentary. *Peabody Journal of Education, 78*(1), 54–67.

Hail, D. (2003). *The effects of home schooling on students as measured by standardized test scores.* Unpublished doctoral dissertation, Sam Houston State University, Huntsville, TX.

Haney, W. (1999, May). Unpublished analysis of a teacher survey on the impact of the TAAS test on teaching and learning, Austin, TX.

Hateley, B. G., & Schmidt, W. H. (2001). *A peacock in the land of penguins: A fable about creativity and courage.* San Francisco: Berrett-Koehler.

Hersey, P., & Blanchard, K. (1993). *Management of organizational behavior: Utilizing human resources* (5th ed.). Englewood Cliffs, NJ: Prentice Hall.

Hirsch, E. D. (1996). *The schools we need and why we don't have them.* New York: Doubleday.

House, R. J. (1971). A path goal theory of leader effectiveness. *Administration Science Quarterly, 16,* 321–368.

House, R. J., & Dressler, G. (1974). The path-goal theory of leadership. *Journal of Contemporary Business, 3,* 81–97.

Isaacs, W. (1999). *Dialogue and the art of thinking together.* New York: Currency.

Kanter, R. (2001). *Evolve: Succeeding in the digital culture of tomorrow.* Boston: Harvard Business School Press.

Kim, D. (1995). Managerial practice fields; Infrastructures of a learning organization. In S. Chawla & J. Renesch (Eds.), *Learning organizations: Developing cultures for tomorrow's workplace* (pp. 351–363). Portland, OR: Productivity Press.

Kuhnert, K. (1994). Transforming leadership: Developing people through delegation. In B. Bass & B. Avolio (Eds.), *Improving organizational effectiveness through transformational leadership* (pp. 10–25). Thousand Oaks, CA: Sage.

Lewin, K. (1951). *Field theory in social science: Selected theoretical papers* (D. Cartwright, Ed.). New York: Harper Torchbooks.

Linn, M. (2003). Testing and accountability. Paper presented at the meeting of the National Council of Professors of Educational Administration, Sedona, AZ.

Maeroff, G. (2003). *A classroom of one: How online learning is changing our schools and colleges.* New York: St. Martins Press.

McNeil, L. (2000). *Contradictions of school reform: Educational costs of standardized testing.* New York: Routledge.

Melaville, A., & Blank, M. (1998). *Learning together: The developing field of school–community initiatives.* Flint, MI: Mott Foundation.

Murphy, J. (1999). Changes in preparation programs: Perceptions of department chairs. In J. Murphy and P. Forsyth (Eds.), *Educational administration: A decade of reform* (pp. 170–190). Thousand Oaks, CA: Corwin Press.

National Center for Education Statistics. (2002, June 6). *National Post-Secondary Student Aid Study.* Washington, DC: U.S. Department of Education, National Center for Education Statistics.

National Commission on Excellence in Education. (1983). *A nation at risk: The imperatives for educational reform.* Washington, DC: U.S. Department of Education.

Northouse, P. (2004). *Leadership: Theory and practice* (3rd ed.). London: Sage.

Ouchi, W. (2003, September 3). Making schools work: The seven keys to success. *Education Week.*

Ouchi, W., & Segal, L. (2003). *Making schools work.* New York: Simon & Schuster.

Palloff, R., & Pratt, K. (2003). *The virtual student: A profile and guide to working with online learners.* San Francisco: Jossey-Bass.

Papalewis, R. (2000). Asynchronous partners: Leadership for the new millennium. *Journal of the Intermountain Center for Educational Effectiveness, 1*(1), 33–39.

Paso, R. (2003). *Capital and opportunity.* New York: University Press.

Peterson, K., & Wimpleberg, R. (1983). *Dual imperatives of principals' work.* Paper presented at the meeting of the American Educational Research Association, Montreal, Quebec, Canada.

Porter, M. (1996). *On competition.* Boston: Harvard Business Review Series.

President's Advisory Committee on Educational Excellence for Hispanic
     Americans. (2000). Report by the Assessment Committee, retrieved
     from www.ed.gov/legislation/FedRegister/other/2002-3/072202b
     .html
Sarason, S. (1999). *Teaching as a performing art.* New York: Teachers
     College Press.
Schweitzer, A. (1963). *Out of my life and thought.* New York: New
     American Library.
Secretary Paige suggests apartheid. (2003, September 9). *Houston
     Chronicle,* p. 9.
Steinberg, S. (2000). *Race and ethnicity in the United States: Issues and
     debates.* Malden, MA: Blackwell.
Stogdill, R. (1948). Personal factors associated with leadership. A
     survey of the literature. *Journal of Psychology, 25,* 35–71.
The Education Resources Institute. (1996, October). *Life after forty.*
     Washington, DC: The Institute of Higher Education Policy.
Ubben, G., & Hughes, L. (2000). *The principal: Creative leadership for
     effective schools.* Needham Heights, MA: Allyn & Bacon.
U.S. Department of Education. (2001). *No Child Left Behind Act.*
     Washington, DC: Author.
Vaill, P. (1989). *Managing as a performing art.* San Francisco: Jossey-Bass.
Waite, D., Boone, M., & McGhee, M. (2001). A critical sociocultural
     view of accountability. *Journal of School Leadership, 11,* 182–201.
     Langham, MD: Scarecrow Press.

# *Index*

Page references followed by *fig* indicate an illustrated figure; followed by *t* indicates a table.

**CORWIN PRESS**

The Corwin Press logo—a raven striding across an open book— represents the union of courage and learning. Corwin Press is committed to improving education for all learners by publishing books and other professional development resources for those serving the field of K–12 education. By providing practical, hands-on materials, Corwin Press continues to carry out the promise of its motto: **"Helping Educators Do Their Work Better."**